No Little People is published in England
as *Ash Heap Lives* (Norfolk Press).

Other books by Francis A. Schaeffer

Escape from Reason
The God Who Is There
Death in the City
Pollution and the Death of Man
The Church at the End of the 20th Century
The Mark of the Christian
The Church before the Watching World
He Is There and He Is Not Silent
True Spirituality
Genesis in Space and Time
The New Super-Spirituality
Back to Freedom and Dignity
Basic Bible Studies
Art and the Bible
Two Contents, Two Realities
Everybody Can Know (Francis & Edith Schaeffer)

Francis A. Schaeffer

No Little People

Sixteen Sermons
for the
Twentieth Century

InterVarsity Press
Downers Grove,
Illinois 60515

Second printing
April 1975

© *1974*
by L'Abri Fellowship.
All rights reserved.
No part of this book may be
reproduced in any form without
written permission from
InterVarsity Press.

InterVarsity Press is the book
publishing division of Inter-Varsity
Christian Fellowship.

The poem "To eat, to breathe . . ."
by Francis A. Schaeffer first
appeared in Christianity Today,
June 20, 1960. Copyright © *1960*
by Christianity Today; *used by*
permission.

ISBN: 0-87784-765-7
Library of Congress Catalog
Card Number: 74-78675

Printed in the United
States of America

To three more very good friends:
Ranald John, Francis and Naomi

Contents

Publisher's Foreword

The ministry of L'Abri Fellowship in Switzerland, where the author has lived and worked for twenty-five years, is multi-faceted. There are lectures in the evenings, discussions—both scheduled and unscheduled throughout each day—times specially set aside for prayer and waiting on the Lord, and times for working. It is a full-orbed life of men and women, families and guests, students and travelers living together, sharing and learning and working—and worshiping the Lord.

Out of this experience come the sixteen sermons of this book. All of them were delivered in the chapel which serves as the worship and study center of L'Abri. Many have also been given during speaking engagements which in recent years have taken the author throughout Europe and to many countries around the world.

These sermons represent a wide variety of styles. Some, like the title sermon, are topical; some expound Old Testament passages, some New Testament passages. Some are weighted toward theology and doctrine, others toward daily life and the practice of Christian faith. But, because the author is both a student of Scripture and a student of contemporary culture, each of these messages is truly for the twentieth century.

Each sermon is a unit written to be read at a single sitting. In fact, we suggest that no more than one be read at a time.

And try reading them aloud. Some are especially useful for reading to families or other groups gathered for Bible study and worship. A church without a pastor may find the sermons a real help in morning worship.

To eat, to breathe
to beget
Is this all there is
Chance configuration of atom against atom
        of god against god
I cannot believe it.
Come, Christian Triune God who lives,
Here am I
Shake the world again.

I

No Little People, No Little Places

As a Christian considers the possibility of being *the Christian glorified* (a topic I have discussed in *True Spirituality*), often his reaction is, "I am so limited. Surely it does not matter much whether I am walking as a creature glorified or not." Or, to put it in another way, "It is wonderful to be a Christian, but I am such a small person, so limited in talents—or energy or psychological strength or knowledge—that what I do is not really important."

The Bible, however, has quite a different emphasis: With God there are no little people.

Moses' Rod

One thing that has encouraged me, as I have wrestled with such questions in my own life, is the way God used Moses' rod, a stick of wood. Many years ago, when I was a young pastor just out of seminary, this study of the use of Moses' rod, which I called "God so used a stick of wood," was a crucial factor in giving me the courage to press on.

The story of Moses' rod began when God spoke to Moses from the burning bush, telling him to go and challenge Egypt, the greatest power of his day. Moses reacted, "Who am I, that I should go unto Pharaoh and that I should bring forth the children of Israel out of Egypt?" (Ex. 3:11), and he raised several specific objections: "They will not believe me, nor harken unto my voice, for they will say, The LORD hath not appeared unto thee. And the LORD said unto him, What is that in thine hand? and he said, A rod" (Ex. 4:1-2). God directed Moses' attention to the simplest thing imaginable—the staff in his own hand, a shepherd's rod, a stick of wood somewhere between three and six feet long.

Shepherds are notorious for hanging onto their staves as long as they can, just as some of us enjoy keeping walking sticks. Moses probably had carried this same staff for years. Since he had been a shepherd in the wilderness for forty years, it is entirely possible that this wood had been dead that long. Just a stick of wood—but when Moses obeyed God's command to toss it on the ground, it became a serpent, and Moses himself fled from it. God next ordered him to take it by the tail and, when he did so, it became a rod again. Then God told him to go and confront the power of Egypt and meet Pharaoh face to face with this rod in his hand.

Exodus 4:20 tells us the secret of all that followed: *The rod of Moses had become the rod of God.*

Standing in front of Pharaoh, Aaron cast down this rod and it became a serpent. As God spoke to Moses and Aaron was the spokesman of Moses (Ex. 4:16), so it would seem that Aaron used the rod of Moses which had become the rod of God. The wizards of Egypt, performing real magic through the power of the devil not just a stage trick through sleight of hand, matched this. Here was demonic power. But the rod of God swallowed up the other rods. This was not merely a victory of Moses over Pharaoh but of Moses' God over Pharaoh's god and the power of the devil behind that god.

This rod appeared frequently in the ensuing events:

Get thee unto Pharaoh in the morning; lo, he goeth out unto the water; and thou shalt stand by the river's brink against he come; and the rod which was turned to a serpent shalt thou take in thine hand. And thou shalt say unto him, The LORD God of the Hebrews hath sent me unto thee, saying, Let my people go, that they may serve me in the wilderness: and, behold, hitherto thou wouldst not hear. Thus saith the LORD, in this thou shalt know that I am the LORD: behold, I will smite with the rod that is in mine hand upon the waters which are in the river, and they shall be turned to blood. (Ex. 7:15-17)

The rod of God indeed was in Aaron's hand (Ex. 7:17, **15** 19-20) and the water was putrefied, an amazing use for a mere stick of wood. In the days that followed, Moses "stretched forth his rod" and successive plagues came upon the land; after the waters no longer were blood, after seven days, there came frogs, then lice, then thunder and hail and great balls of ball lightning running along the ground, and then locusts (Ex. 8:1—10:15). Watch the destruction of judgment, which came from a dead stick of wood that had become the rod of God.

Pharaoh's grip on the Hebrews was shaken loose, and he let the people go. But then he changed his mind and ordered his armies to pursue them. When the armies came upon them, the Hebrews were caught in a narrow place with mountains on one side of them and the sea on the other. And God said to Moses, "Lift thou up thy rod" (Ex. 14:16). What good is it to lift up a rod when one is caught in a cul-de-sac between mountains and a great body of water with the mightiest army in the world at his heels? Much good, if the rod is the rod of God. The waters divided and the people passed through. Up to this point, the rod had been used for judgment and destruction, but now it was a rod of healing for the Jews, as it was the rod of judgment for the Egyptians. That which is in the hand of God can be used in either way.

Later, the rod of judgment also became a rod of supply. In Rephidim the people desperately needed water.

And the LORD said unto Moses, Go on before the people, and take with thee of the elders of Israel; and thy rod, wherewith thou smotest the river, take in thine hand, and go. Behold, I will stand before thee there upon the rock in Horeb; and thou shalt smite the rock, and there shall come water out of it, that the people may drink. And Moses did so in the sight of the elders of Israel. (Ex. 17:5-6)

It must have been an amazing sight to stand before a great rock (not a small pebble but a face of rock such as we see here in Switzerland in the mountains) and to see a rod struck against it, and then to watch torrents of life-giving water flow out to satisfy thousands upon thousands of people and their livestock. The giver of judgment became the giver of life. It was not magic. There was nothing in the rod itself. The rod of Moses had simply become the rod of God. We too are not only to speak a word of judgment to our lost world, but are also to be a source of life.

The rod also brought military victory as it was held up. It was more powerful than the swords of either the Jews or their enemy (Ex. 17:9). In a much later incident the people revolted against Moses, and a test was established to see whom God had indeed chosen. The rod was placed before God and it budded (Num. 17:8). Incidentally, we find out what kind of tree it had come from so long ago because it now brought forth almond blossoms.

The final use of the rod occurred when the wilderness wandering was almost over. Moses' sister Miriam had already died. Forty years had passed since the people had left Egypt, so now the rod may have been almost eighty years old. The people again needed water, and, though they were now in a different place, the desert of Zin, they were still murmuring against God. So God told Moses,

> Take the rod, and gather thou the assembly together, thou, and Aaron thy brother, and speak ye unto the rock before their eyes; and it shall give forth his water, and thou shalt bring forth to them water out of the rock: so thou shalt give the congregation and their beasts drink. And Moses took the rod from before the LORD, as he commanded him. (Num. 20:8-9)

Moses took the rod (which verse 9 with 17:10 shows was the same one which had been kept with the arc since it had budded) and he struck the rock twice. He should have done what God had told him and only spoken with the rod in his hand, but that is another study. In spite of this, however, "water came out abundantly" (Num. 20:11).

Consider the mighty ways in which God used a dead stick of wood. "God so used a stick of wood" can be a banner cry for each of us. Though we are limited and weak in talent, physical energy and psychological strength, we are not less than a stick of wood. But as the rod of Moses had to become the rod of God, so that which is *me* must become the *me* of God. Then, I can become useful in God's hands. The Scripture emphasizes that much can come from little if the little is truly consecrated to God. There are no little people and no big people in the true spiritual sense, but only consecrated and unconsecrated people. The problem for each of us is applying this truth to ourselves: Is Francis Schaeffer the Francis Schaeffer of God?

No Little Places

But if a Christian is consecrated, does this mean he will be in a big place instead of a little place? The answer, the next step, is very important: As there are no little people in God's sight, so there are no little places. To be wholly committed to God in the place where God wants him— this is the creature glorified. In my writing and lecturing I put much emphasis on God's being the infinite reference point which integrates the intellectual problems of life. He is to be this, but he must be the reference point not only in our thinking but in our living. This means being what he wants me to be, where he wants me to be.

Nowhere more than in America are Christians caught in the twentieth-century syndrome of size. Size will show success. If I am consecrated, there will necessarily be large quantities of people, dollars, etc. This is not so. Not only does God not say that size and spiritual power go together, but he even reverses this (especially in the teaching of Jesus) and tells us to be deliberately careful not to choose a place too big for us. We all tend to emphasize big works and big places, but all such emphasis is of the flesh. To think in such terms is simply to hearken back to the old, unconverted, egoist, self-centered *Me*. This attitude, taken from the world, is more dangerous to the Christian than fleshly amusement or practice. It is the flesh.

People in the world naturally want to boss others. Imagine a boy beginning work with a firm. He has a lowly place and is ordered around by everyone: Do this! Do that! Every dirty job is his. He is the last man on the totem pole, merely one of Rabbit's friends-and-relations, in Christopher Robin's terms. So one day when the boss is out, he enters the boss's office, looks around carefully to see that no one is there and then sits down in the boss's big chair. "Someday," he says, "I'll say 'run' and they'll run." This is man. And let us say with tears that a person does not automatically abandon this mentality when he becomes a Christian. In every one of us there remains a seed of wanting to be boss, of wanting to be in control and have the word of power over our fellows. But the Word of God teaches us that we are to have a very different mentality:

> But Jesus called them [his disciples] to him, and saith unto them, Ye know that they which are accounted to rule over the Gentiles lord it over them; and their great ones exercise authority upon them. But so shall it not be among you: but whosoever will be great among you, shall be your minister: And whosoever of you will be the chiefest, shall be servant of all. For even the Son of man came not to be ministered unto, but to minister, and to give his life a ransom for many. (Mk. 10:42-45)

Every Christian, without exception, is called into the place where Jesus stood. To the extent that we are called to leadership, we are called to ministry, even costly ministry. The greater the leadership, the greater is to be the ministry. The word *minister* is not a title of power but a designation of servanthood. There is to be no Christian guru. We must reject this constantly and carefully. A minister, a man who is a leader in the church of God (and never more needed than in a day like ours when the battle is so great) *must* make plain to the men, women, boys and girls who come to places of leadership that instead of lording their authority over others and allowing it to become an ego trip, they are to serve in humility.

Again, Jesus said, "But be not ye called Rabbi: for one is your Master, even Christ; and all ye are brethren" (Mt. 23:8). This does not mean there is to be no order in the church. It does mean that the *basic* relationship between Christians is not that of elder and people, or pastor and people, but that of brothers and sisters in Christ. This denotes that there is one Father in the family and that his offspring are equal. There are different jobs to be done, different offices to be filled, but we as Christians are equal before one Master. We are not to seek a great title; we are to have the places together as brethren.

When Jesus said, "He that is greatest among you shall be your servant" (Mt. 23:11), he was not speaking in hyperbole or uttering a romantic idiom. Jesus Christ is the realist of all realists, and when he says this to us, he is telling us something specific we are to do.

Our attitude toward all men should be that of equality because we are common creatures. We are of one blood and kind. As I look across all the world, I must see every man as a fellow creature and I must be careful to have a sense of our equality on the basis of this common status. We must be careful in our thinking not to try to stand in the place of God to other men. We are fellow creatures.

20 And when I step from the creature-to-creature relationship into the brothers-and-sisters-in-Christ relationship within the church, how much more important to be a brother or sister to all who have the same Father. Orthodoxy, to be a Bible-believing Christian, always has two faces. It has a creedal face and a practicing face, and Christ emphasizes that that is to be the case here. Dead orthodoxy is always a contradiction in terms and clearly that is so here; to be a Bible-believing Christian demands humility regarding others in the body of Christ.

Jesus gave us a tremendous example:

Jesus knowing that the Father had given all things into his hands, and that he was come from God, and went to God; He riseth from supper, and laid aside his garments; and took a towel, and girded himself. After that he poureth water into a bason, and began to wash the disciples' feet, and to wipe them with the towel wherewith he was girded. . . . Ye call me Master and Lord: and ye say well; for so I am. If I then, your Lord and Master, have washed your feet; ye also ought to wash one another's feet. For I have given you an example, that ye should do as I have done to you. Verily, verily, I say unto you, The servant is not greater than his lord; neither he that is sent greater than he that sent him. If ye know these things, happy are ye if ye do them. (John 13:3-5, 13-17)

Note that Jesus says that if we do these things there will be happiness. It is not just knowing these things that brings happiness, it is doing them. Throughout Jesus' teaching these two words *know* and *do* occur constantly, and always in that order. We cannot do until we know, but we can know without doing. The house built on the rock is the house of the man who knows and does. The house built on the sand is the house of the man who knows but does not do.

Christ washed the disciples' feet and dried them with the towel with which he was girded, that is, with his own clothing. He intended this to be a practical example of the mentality and action that should be seen in the midst of the people of God.

Taking the Lowest Place

Yet another statement of Jesus bears on our discussion:

And he put forth a parable to those which were bidden, when he marked how they chose out the chief rooms; saying unto them, When thou art bidden of any man to a wedding, sit not down in the highest room; lest a more honourable man than thou be bidden of him; And he that bade thee and him come and say to thee, Give this man place; and thou begin with shame to take the lowest room. But when thou art bidden, go and sit down in the lowest room; that when he that bade thee cometh, he may say unto thee, Friend, go up higher: then shalt thou have worship in the presence of them that sit at meat with thee. For

21

whosoever exalteth himself shall be abased; and he that humbleth himself shall be exalted. (Lk. 14:7-11)

Jesus commands Christians to seek consciously the lowest room. All of us—pastors, teachers, professional religious workers and non-professional included—are tempted to say, "I will take the larger place because it will give me more influence for Jesus Christ." Both individual Christians and Christian organizations fall prey to the temptation of rationalizing this way as we build bigger and bigger empires. But according to the Scripture this is backwards: We should consciously take the lowest place unless the Lord himself extrudes us into a greater one.

The word *extrude* is important here. To be extruded is to be forced out under pressure into a desired shape. Picture a huge press jamming soft metal at high pressure through a die so that the metal comes out in a certain shape. This is the way of the Christian: He should choose the lesser place until God extrudes him into a position of more responsibility and authority.

Let me suggest two reasons why we ought not grasp the larger place. First, we should seek the lowest place because there it is easier to be quiet before the face of the Lord. I did not say easy; in no place, no matter how small or humble, is it easy to be quiet before God. But it is certainly easier in some places than in others. And the little places, where I can more easily be close to God, should be my preference. I am not saying that it is impossible to be quiet before God in a greater place, but God must be allowed to choose when a Christian is ready to be extruded into such a place, for only he knows when a person will be able to have some quietness before him in the midst of increased pressure and responsibility.

Quietness and peace before God are more important than any influence a position may seem to give, for we must stay in step with God to have the power of the Holy Spirit. If by taking a bigger place our quietness with God is lost, then to that extent our fellowship with him is broken and we are living in the flesh, and the final result will not be as great, no matter how important the larger place may look in the eyes of other men or in our own eyes. Always there will be a battle, always we will be less than perfect, but if a place is too big and too active for our present spiritual condition, then it is too big.

We see this happen over and over again and perhaps it has happened at some time to us: Someone whom God has been using marvelously in a certain place takes it upon himself to move into a larger place and loses his quietness with God. Ten years later he may have a huge organization, but the power has gone, and he is no longer a real part of the battle in his generation. The final result of not being quiet before God is that less will be done, not more—no matter how much Christendom may be beating its drums or playing its trumpets for a particular activity.

23

So we must not go out beyond our depth. Take the smaller place so you have quietness before God. I am not talking about laziness; let me make that clear. That is something else, something too which God hates. I am not talking about copping out or dropping out. God's people are to be active, not seeking, on account of some false mystical concept, to sit constantly in the shade of a rock. There is no monasticism in Christianity. We will not be lazy in our relationship with God, because when the Holy Spirit burns, a man is consumed. We can expect to become physically tired in the midst of battle for our King and Lord; we should not expect all of life to be a vacation. We are talking about quietness before God as we are in his place for us. The size of the place is not important but the consecration in that place is.

It must be noted that all these things which are true for

an individual are true also for a group. A group can become activistic and take on responsibilities God has not laid upon it. For both the individual and the group the first reason we are not to grasp (and the emphasis is on *grasp*) the larger place is that we must not lose our quietness with God.

The second reason why we should not seek the larger place is that if we deliberately and egotistically lay hold on leadership, wanting the drums to beat and the trumpets to blow, then we are not qualified for Christian leadership. Why? Because we have forgotten that we are brothers and sisters in Christ with other Christians. I have said on occasion that there is only one good kind of fighter for Jesus Christ—the man who does not like to fight. The belligerent man is never the one to be belligerent for Jesus. And it is exactly the same with leadership. The Christian leader should be a quiet man of God who is extruded by God's grace into some place of leadership.

24

We all have egoistic pressures inside us. We may have substantial victories over them and we may grow, but we never completely escape them in this life. The pressure is always there deep in my heart and soul, needing to be faced with honesty. These pressures are evident in the smallest of things as well as the greatest. I have seen fights over who was going to be the president of a Sunday school class composed of three members. The temptation has nothing to do with size. It comes from a spirit, a mentality, inside us. The person in leadership for leadership's sake is returning to the way of the world, like the boy dusting off the boss's chair and saying, "Someday I'll sit in it, and I'll make people jump."

One of the loveliest incidents in the early church occurred when Barnabas concluded that Paul was the man of the hour and then had to seek him out because Paul had gone back to Tarsus, his own little place. Paul was not up there nominating himself; he was back in

Tarsus, even out of communication as far as we can tell. When Paul called himself "the chief of sinners, . . . not meet to be an apostle" (1 Tim. 1:15; 1 Cor. 15:9), he was not speaking just for outward form's sake. From what he said elsewhere and from his actions we can see that this was Paul's mentality. Paul, the man of leadership for the whole Gentile world, was perfectly willing to be in Tarsus until God said to him, "This is the moment."

Being a Rod of God

The people who receive praise from the Lord Jesus will not in every case be the people who held leadership in this life. There will be many persons who were sticks of wood that stayed close to God and were quiet before him, and were used in power by him in a place which looks small to men.

Each Christian is to be a rod of God in the place of God for him. We must remember throughout our lives that in God's sight there are no little people and no little places. Only one thing is important: to be consecrated persons in God's place for us, at each moment. Those who think of themselves as little people in little places, if committed to Christ and living under his Lordship in the whole of life, may, by God's grace, change the flow of our generation. And as we get on a bit in our lives, knowing how weak we are, if we look back and see we have been somewhat used of God, then we should be the rod "surprised by joy."

25

II

The
Hand
of
God

One of the great hymns of the church is "Guide Me, O Thou Great Jehovah," which begins like this:

> Guide me, O thou great Jehovah,
> Pilgrim through this barren land;
> I am weak, but thou art mighty,
> Hold me with thy powerful hand.

The phrase "hold me with thy powerful hand" has been a great comfort and blessing to God's people down through the ages. But I would raise two questions about it: First, does the word *hand* used this way show *primitivism* in the Scripture? Does it demonstrate that the Bible is, after all, an ancient book which from an evolutionary perspective should be viewed as being old-fashioned in a very basic way? Second, is it just *romanticism*, merely a poetic expression that gives God's people *only* emotional comfort?

God Is Spirit

The Bible says plainly that God is a pure Spirit and does not literally have a hand. That we are made in the image of God does not mean that God has feet, eyes and hands like ours.

Nor does God need a hand, for in the greatest of all acts, the creation of all things out of nothing, he merely *spoke and it was* (Ps. 33:9), the most dynamic and overflowing short phrase in all of language. Psalm 148 has a parallel statement: "He commanded, and they were created" (v. 5). The whole Bible makes it plain that in this titanic beginning of all things, God who is Spirit created by divine fiat. He willed, he spoke and all things came into existence.

If God does not literally have a hand, then why does the Scripture use this expression? The answer is simple. God wants us to know him as *personal*. He wants to communicate to us in propositional, verbalized form the reality of his personality working in history. And how can he do this? By making use of the tremendous parallels between us finite men, created in God's image, and God himself.

What do hands mean to us men? Hands equal action. The hands are that part of a man which produces something in the external world. We move always from our thought world outward. As men, we think, we have emotions and we will. The artist desiring to paint a picture, the engineer desiring to build a bridge, the housewife desiring to bake a cake—each must do more than mere thinking and willing. Action must flow from the thought world of the inward man out through his hands into the external world which confronts him.

If a business letter must be typed, hands upon the typewriter produce it. If we are digging in our garden in the spring or fall, our hands hold the spade. If a poet wants to write a poem, his hand guides the pen. In warfare, the hand holds the sword. In each case, man projects the wonder of his personality—his thoughts, his emotions and the determinations of his will—into a historic, space-time world through the use of his body, and especially his hands.

So in order to communicate to us that he is a personal God who acts into space-time history, God uses the image of "the hand of God." It is a familiar phrase, easily understood. But there is nothing primitive about this way of speaking. He uses this term which we know in order that we might understand exactly what he is saying. Nor does God use this expression in a poetic, romantic way merely so that we can feel better when we think of it. Rather, he is telling us an overwhelming yet basic truth: that he, without physical hands, can equal and surpass in space-time history all that we men can do with physical hands.

Now let us consider several ways God uses his 29 "hand."

The Hand of God Creates
As we have already mentioned, God uses his hand to create: "Hearken unto me, O Jacob and Israel, my called; I am he; I am the first, I also am the last. Mine hand also hath laid the foundation of the earth, and my right hand hath spanned the heavens: when I call unto them, they stand up together" (Is. 48:12-13). In this tremendous picture, we see that the hand of God is no puny thing either in the past at the creation or in the present.

We have in Isaiah's brief statement almost an entire theology of God, a whole system concerning who God is. First, he is transcendent. Because he is the Creator of the external world, he is not caught in it; he is above his creation. This stands in contrast to modern theology with its pure immanence. But, second, he is not transcendent in the sense of being the philosophic other or the impersonal everything. He is also truly immanent.

Though he is transcendent, he still can and does work in the universe. And it is important in a day like our own to understand this relationship between God and the machine. The universe exists because God made it, and he made it to work on a cause-and-effect basis. But it is not controlled entirely by the uniformity of natural causes in a closed system. God has made the machine, but he can work into it anytime he wills.

On the one hand, then, cause-and-effect relationships exist. Without them there would be no science, there would be nothing we could know. It is not just arbitrary actions on the part of God that make the tree grow, the snow come, the rain fall. And yet, at the same time, God is not caught within these cause-and-effect relationships. He is not part of the machine. He has made it and can act into it anytime he wishes.

30 This theology of God and his relation to the world is emphasized often in Isaiah. For instance, we read in Isaiah 45: "I have made the earth, and created man upon it: I, even my hands, have stretched out the heavens, and all their host have I commanded" (Is. 45:12). God has not made a little universe. He has made the wide stretches of space and has put there all the flaming hosts we see at night, all the planets, stars and galaxies. Wherever we go let us remind ourselves that God has made everything we see.

No matter what man eventually discovers the universe to be, no matter how much it contains or how great its stretch, this man must know—that God made it all. And not only did God make it all, but he is present to work in any part of it at any time he wishes. There is no place in the far-flung universe where the hand of God cannot work.

The entire Old Testament cries out that God is not a localized God, not a God of one part of the land, nor a

God who dwells only in the temple, nor a God who is carried in the box of the ark. He is the God who dwells in the heavens and does what he wills. "Of old hast thou laid the foundation of the earth: and the heavens are the work of thy hands," the psalmist affirms (Ps. 102:25).

The Hand of God Preserves

In addition to declaring that God is the Creator of the entire universe, the Bible also makes clear that he did not create the earth and then walk away. His hand also operates to preserve his creation, both conscious and unconscious life: "That thou givest them they gather: thou openest thine hand, they are filled with good" (Ps. 104:28). And again, "The eyes of all wait upon thee; and thou givest them their food in due season. Thou openest thine hand, and satisfiest the desire of every living thing" (Ps. 145:15-16).

Nothing lives in a vacuum. Everything in the world is preserved by God on its own level. Machines, plants, animals, men, angels—God preserves each one existentially, moment by moment, on its own level. Can we use our hands to work in the external world? God works in the external world.

An antiphonal doxology in the psalms praises God for being a worker in the creation he has made:

O give thanks unto the Lord; for he is good:
for his mercy endureth for ever.
O give thanks unto the God of gods:
for his mercy endureth for ever.
O give thanks to the Lord of lords:
for his mercy endureth for ever.
To him who alone doeth great wonders:
for his mercy endureth for ever. (Ps. 136:1-4)

The succeeding verses praise God for specific actions. One is that God "brought Israel out from among them [the Egyptians] . . . with a strong hand, and with a stretched out arm" (vv. 11-12). Not just a generalized statement about preservation, this mentions a specific event—the Jews' deliverance from Egypt. Praise is being given here because God is a worker in the creation he has made. The Jews always looked back to this work that God had done in space and time, and therefore they were linked to something that was tough enough to bear the weight of life, for they knew that God was not far away. Their affirmation was not just a poetic expression. Since God had acted in past history, the people knew they could trust him for the future.

After God had brought many plagues upon Egypt, the court magicians had said to Pharaoh, "This is the finger of God" (Ex. 8:19). During the earliest plagues, the magicians undoubtedly had thought that these might be chance occurrences or that by using the power of the demons they themselves would be able to duplicate the plagues. But as they watched the increasing horror of the plagues, these magicians came to another conclusion: This is more than chance, or, to speak in modern terms, this is more than the machine, more than merely cause and effect in a closed system. They concluded that there was a God who was acting in history. They admitted, "This is the finger of God."

God's acting in history is also portrayed forcefully in the giving of the Ten Commandments soon after the Jews left Egypt. The scene is described this way: "And he gave unto Moses, when he had made an end of communing with him upon mount Sinai, two tables of testimony, tables of stone, written with the finger of God" (Ex. 31:18). God took two blank tables of stone (we are not sure what they looked like; we think we do because of the way the artists have painted them for so many centuries, but we really do not) and then, either gradually or suddenly, carved on them the words he wanted there.

If Michelangelo had wanted to chisel words on these tables, he would have placed the tables in his studio, fastened them properly, taken his favorite hammer and chisel (which he would have made lovingly with his own hands, as sculptors did in those days) and worked away. With one hand holding the chisel and the other the hammer, he gradually would have produced words on the stone, and beautifully carved ones, I am sure. Out of his own thought world whatever he would have wanted to put on the tables would have appeared—his personality would have flowed through his fingers into the external world.

And that is exactly what God did on Mount Sinai. As Moses looked at the tables of stone with nothing on them, words appeared. But God did not need physical hands or a chisel. He who spoke all things into existence had only to will, and, in the historic, space-time world, words appeared on stone.

God speaks to men through verbalization, using natural syntax and grammar, as when, on the Damascus road, Jesus spoke to Paul in the Hebrew tongue. He did not use a "heavenly language." Both on the Damascus road and on Mount Sinai, God used regular verbalization—and the syntax was good, let us be sure. And both events affirm, let us stress again, that God is able to work into the machine any time he will.

Here is the distinction we must see between existential theology, Greek thought and Jewish thought. Modern existential theology says, "Truth is all in your head. You must make a leap, completely removed from the common things of life." The Greeks were tougher than this, for they said, "If you're going to have truth, it has to make sense." If a man would insist, as modern man does, "I will believe these things whether they make sense or not," the Greek philosopher would answer, "That is foolish. A system which is internally inconsist-

ent is unacceptable." So the Greeks were better than
modern man in his modern theology.

But the Jews were stronger yet. The Jews said, "Yes,
truth must fit together in a system that is noncontradic-
tory, but it must do something more. It must be rooted
in the space-time stuff of history." The Jews throughout
their history affirmed that God's hand had done a great
thing in releasing them from Egypt. Therefore, they
were not shaken in the midst of trial because they knew
what God could do in the external world.

The Hand of God Chastises

But God's action in the external world can be even more
personal than it was when he led the Jews out of Egypt.
We Christians should be grateful for that event, which,
since we are spiritual Jews, is part of our history.
It should be our environment to offset the environment
of our own day when men are seen as only machines.
But God can be even more personal. He can and does
say, "I use my hand *for you*."

One way God expresses his fatherly care for his children is in loving chastisement. How do parents spank
their children? They use their hand. Similarly, when one
of his children needs chastisement, God brings down
his hand.

In Psalm 32:4, for instance, David says, "For day and
night thy hand was heavy upon me," or, in other words,
"You have chastened me." In Psalm 39:10, David cries,
"Remove thy stroke away from me: I am consumed by
the blow of thine hand."

This chastisement was not merely psychological, another important truth for our generation to understand.
The hand of God is pictured as working not in the
thoughts of men but into the external world. He uses the
word *hand* so that we have perfect communication: That
which we use our hands to do, he, being a personal

God, accomplishes without hands. One such action is chastisement.

The chastisement of David for his sin with Bathsheba was not just psychological. In this and in other pictures of chastisement in the Bible God did not do something inside the heads of men. Rather, in his loving care for his people, he chastened them through external situations. God worked into the machine not only to achieve the mighty exodus from Egypt, not only to carve his law upon the rock, but also to show love to his people by chastening them. God is not far off, acting only in the great moments of history; he is acting into our own personal history in a loving way as well.

The Hand of God Cares for His People

God does not apply his hand only to chastise. He uses it to care for his people, too. The human hand has an amazing quality that nothing else has: tremendous efficiency of strength and yet total gentleness. (The nearest thing to it, incidentally, is an elephant's trunk, but that does not come very close!) A hand is extremely strong for its size, and yet it can be most gentle. There is nothing as gentle as a lover's hand. Thus, the hand of God can shake the world, but it can also express tenderness and love toward his individual children.

Sometimes we act as if God is the philosophic other or the impersonal everything, in short, as if he is only a word. The psalmist describes the wicked man who really believes this: "He hath said in his heart, God hath forgotten: he hideth his face; he will never see it" (Ps. 10:11). But the psalmist follows this with a contrasting statement: "Arise, O LORD; O God, lift up thine hand" (Ps. 10:12). With these imperatives, he is saying to God: "Act in the world to show people you exist. Show them that you can work in history, that you are not far off." Then he cries, "Lift up thine hand: forget not the humble. Wherefore doth the wicked contemn God? He hath said in his heart, Thou wilt not require it. Thou hast seen it; for thou beholdest mischief and spite, to requite it with thy hand: the poor committeth himself unto thee; thou art the helper of the fatherless" (Ps. 10:12-14). Let us never forget that in our poor world we are all fatherless, some more obviously so than others. But since God is immanent we can all cry to him.

Another psalm plays on the word *hand*: "My times are in thy hand: deliver me from the hand of mine enemies, and from them that persecute me" (Ps. 31:15). The first clause of this verse, "My times are in thy hand," expresses the realization, as up to date as tomorrow's theological and philosophical discussion, that we live in a universe which we can speak of as personal, one which does not trap God in its machinery.

The second clause compares the hand of God to the hand of men. Men can take their hands and slap me across the face; they can tie me down and beat me. "O God," the psalmist asks, "I often fall into the hands of men, but, O God, I put myself into your hand in the midst of the present space-time history."

Psalm 37 expresses the same confidence in God's care: "Though he [the righteous] fall, he shall not be utterly cast down: for the LORD upholdeth him with his hand. I have been young, and now am old; yet have I not seen the righteous forsaken, nor his seed begging bread" (Ps. 37:24-25). The psalmist sees, as he reviews the past, that the Lord holds his own in his hand. This is not just a psychological projection, a blind leap in the dark, an upper-story experience which is not open to verification. It is the very opposite. We can look into the world and see God acting for his individual people through the might of his hand. A beautiful perspective, which suddenly changes the world. Instead of living in the modern consensus, surrounded by the impersonal, I live in a personal environment and am more than a speck tossed to and fro by impersonal chance.

But don't the wicked often do well, too? Don't the affluent wicked number in the millions today? The psalmist wrestled with this: "But as for me, my feet were almost gone; my steps had well nigh slipped. For I was envious at the foolish, when I saw the prosperity of the wicked" (Ps. 73:2-3). But he reached this conclusion: "So foolish was I, and ignorant: I was as a beast before thee. Nevertheless I am continually with thee: thou hast holden me by my right hand. Thou shalt guide me with thy counsel, and afterward receive me to glory. Whom have I in heaven but thee? . . . God is . . . my portion forever" (Ps. 73:22-26).

In the last clause of this quote, we see that the psalmist knows something else about God's care for his children: It does not end at death. It carries them into a future beyond death. The affluent wicked will perish, but God 37 will act on behalf of his child not only now but forever.

And as I raise my eyes and look at the environment surrounding me, it looks different. I live in a personal world, and God is dealing with me not for a few short years but forever. And I can make different value judgments as I look at the world because I understand that reality does not exist only between birth and death. A personal God is acting in a true history that goes on forever.

Not only does God care for his people throughout all time, he also can express his love for them no matter where they are located: "If I take the wings of the morning, and dwell in the uttermost parts of the sea; Even there shall thy hand lead me, and thy right hand shall hold me" (Ps. 139:9-10). Conversely, the lost man cannot make his own universe even in hell, for "if I make my bed in hell, behold, thou art there" (Ps. 139:8). And this, I suppose, is the center of the hellishness of hell, that the rebel cannot make his own universe even there. But the same thing holds true for the people of God. As a child of God, I cannot go anywhere where God is not present to hold my hand.

In Psalm 143, David muses on God's working in history: "I remember the days of old; I meditate on all thy works; I muse on the work of thy hands" (Ps. 143:5). And he sees that on the basis of God's past activity he himself can do something in the present, existential moment: "I stretch forth my hands unto thee: my soul thirsteth after thee, as a thirsty land" (Ps. 143:6). David paints a marvelous picture here. As a person looks back at God's actions in history and makes this his own environment, then he can have a positive reaction in this existential moment: As God's child, he can raise his hands in personal confidence. This is the walk of the Christian.

38   Why does the boy out hiking with his father reach out his hand when they come to a slippery place? He does it because in the past his father has faithfully taken his outstretched hand, and they have walked over the slippery trails together. This portrays the Christian walk with God, and the picture is beautiful. I raise my hand to my Father in personal relationship, and then walk with him hand in hand.

The Hand of God Provides Security

We can understand even better now why the psalms praise God:

> O come, let us sing unto the LORD: let us make a joyful noise to the rock of our salvation. Let us come before his presence with thanksgiving, and make a joyful noise unto him with psalms. For the LORD is a great God, and a great King above all gods. In his hand are the deep places of the earth: the strength of the hills is his also. The sea is his, and he made it: and his hands

formed the dry land. O come, let us worship and bow down: let us kneel before the LORD our maker. For he is our God; and we are the people of his pasture, and the sheep of his hand. (Ps. 95:1-7) The sheep of his hand! Is that a strange expression? Not at all. At least it should not be strange by this time. It is the shepherd's hand that guides the sheep, the shepherd's hand that takes the crook to rescue the silly sheep and the rod to guard against the wolf that chases the sheep. And we are God's sheep for whom he acts in history.

God has made us a promise: He is committed to work in history for us his sheep. Being his sheep is not just pie in the sky, or a better leap than some other leap, or the relief we get from using evangelical God-words. All these are a kind of blasphemy. That we are his sheep means he works in the external world on our behalf.

Jesus uses the image of the shepherd's hand in exactly **39** the same way: "My sheep hear my voice, and I know them, and they follow me: and I give unto them eternal life; and they shall never perish, neither shall anything pluck them out of my hand" (John 10:27-28). Here we see the tremendous fact that the second Person of the Trinity, because he *is* deity and because of his finished work on Calvary, can say, "When you become my sheep, I will hold you in my hand." The hand of gentleness and power will hold us securely. In order to bring home this truth with even greater force, he even repeats it, making a couplet out of it: "My Father, which gave them to me, is greater than all; and nothing is able to pluck them out of my Father's hand" (John 10:29).

So we are informed about this titanic security of being held in the hand of the Son and in the hand of the Father. Nothing is able to pluck us out, for our Father is greater than all. Without a doubt, when Jesus said this he was not merely using a figure of speech but was fitting his statement into the whole Jewish mentality of a space-time reality based on the expression "the hand of God." He who is able and does work in the machine of the universe of the external world loves us and will work in the universe to protect us, to chasten us when we need it for our care. Nothing is able to pluck us out of God's hand.

The Hand of God Invites
The Jews understood that all these statements about the hand of God were being said in contrast to all the other gods that men have made. The psalmist says that these other gods are not like the living God: "They have hands, but they handle not: feet have they, but they walk not: neither speak they through their throat" (Ps. 115:7). Whether a god is made of stone, wood, gold or silver, or whether it is a projection of the mind of modern men (who make their gods merely in their thoughts), the Bible says there is a great distinction between it and the living God. Such a god (that is, an idol made of stone, wood, etc.) has a hand but cannot do anything with it. He has feet but never takes a step, a mouth and throat but never says a word.

But the true God is not like this. He does not literally have hands, as an idol does, but he is able to work into history any time he wills. He does not have feet, but he will be wherever we need him. Without a mouth he is able to do what men do with theirs, that is, to communicate through verbalization; and he has given us his propositional communication in the Bible.

And through that communication the hand that creates, preserves, chastises, cares for people and provides security, does something else—it invites. God said regarding the Israelites, "I have spread out my hands all the day unto a rebellious people, which walketh in a way that was not good, after their own thoughts" (Is. 65:2). God invites but the rebellious walk in their own thoughts rather than heeding this invitation.

Spreading out one's hands in invitation is a natural gesture. If you watch any natural speaker, he will use it without ever having been taught it. When giving any kind of invitation, he will use his hands. "I do the same," God says. "I stretch out my hands to you. I am constantly extending a sweet invitation, but you hardhearted and rebellious men do not listen to it."

So if you are a non-Christian, I would say to you, Will you respond to the invitation of the outreached hands of God? Will you give yourself to the God who is there, the God who has acted and is acting in history? And I would urge Christians also to remember this invitation. Much of the time we, too, are rebellious people. Aren't we ashamed that even though God stretches out his hand to us day by day we so often turn away?

God's invitation is not a gesture made only now and then. Look at all the verification that God's hands are at **41** work. Look over all God's works in history. Those of you who are children of God, look back in your own personal life and see what God has done. Reach back beyond that into the flow of history. And then remember: The acts of God's hand are a constant invitation for you to come to him, to stop being rebellious and to have him as your real environment.

Ⅲ

The Weakness of God's Servants

I f someone asked us "What is the Bible?" we probably would not begin our answer by saying, "The Bible is a realistic book." Yet in the twentieth century this might be the best place to start—to stress the realism of the Bible in contrast to the romanticism which characterizes the twentieth-century concept of religion. To most modern people, truth is to be sought through some sort of leap from which we extract our own personal religious experiences.

Many feel that the Bible should portray a romantic view of life, but the Bible is actually the most realistic book in the world. It does not glibly say, "God's on his throne; all's well with the world." It faces the world's dilemmas squarely. Yet, unlike modern *realism* which ends in despair, it has answers for the dilemmas. And, unlike modern *romanticism*, its answers are not optimism without a sufficient base, not hope hung in a vacuum.

So we should say at once to twentieth-century people: The Bible is a tough-fibered book.

Force and Form

The Bible's realism leads to many practical applications. For example, because it views men as sinners, the Bible teaches that there is a need for force in this fallen world. Form will not grow by itself. Allen Ginsberg has been typical of some who say that form is unnecessary: Remove form and life will turn out really well. But take a good look at society without form and without at least some force to maintain that form. Anarchy soon dehumanizes men.

But happily the Bible gives answers which fit the structure of a lost world. It teaches that force must be used at many different levels. Christians understand that chastisement must be used at home. If our children are part of the revolted race of men (as the Bible says they are), then in our homes we must provide structure and form as well as freedom. The balance of form and freedom must exist in the home in a practical way: There must be chastisement as a part of love.

The biblical concept is rooted in the character of God himself. God exists and he is holy; he hates sin and wrong and cruelty. He will judge sin, yet at the same time he is love. So the Christian's task is to show forth, and act upon, the character of God. The Christian should not be romantic toward sin and the lostness of the world; in his home, society, church, organizations and relationships, he should implement judgment when necessary—but with the simultaneous motives of righteousness and love.

Once we see the Bible's realism, we can understand why the Reformation produced a democracy of checks and balances. A Christian does not trust even himself with unlimited power. Calvin pointed out that because men are sinners it is better to be governed by the many rather than the few or a single man. Every Christian organization and every state built on the Reformation mentality are built to allow men freedom under God but not unlimited freedom. Unlimited freedom will not work in a lost world; some structure and form are necessary.

So when we say that the Bible is a realistic book, this is not just a theoretical proposition on a metaphysical chess board. It relates to realities in life—realities in the home, in government, in the way we look at the world.

Sin and the Cruelty of Utopianism

Sin is sin, and we must not call it less than sin. It is not an act of love to explain sin away as psychological determinism or sociological conditioning, for it is real and must be dealt with. Men need a Savior. Therefore, Christians in our generation must resist relativistic and 45 deterministic thinking. If men are going to find a real solution to the problem of who they are, they must come to terms with the fact that they need a Savior because they are sinners in the presence of a holy God. Sin is serious business.

Equally as Christians, sin in our lives is also a serious business. We are never merely to explain it away—in ourselves, in our group or in our family.

On the other hand, knowing that all men are sinners frees us from the cruelty of utopianism. Utopianism is cruel for it expects of men and women what they are not and will not be until Christ comes. Such utopianism, forgetting what the Bible says about human sinfulness, is hard-hearted; it is as monstrous a thing as one can imagine.

I have said that sin is a serious business and we must never minimize that. But we are also being less than biblical if we slip into romanticism and utopianism.

Bible-believing Christians should never have the reaction designated by the term *shocked*. There is a type of Christian who constantly draws himself or herself up and declares, "I am shocked." If he is, he is not reacting to reality as he should, for it is as much against the teaching of Scripture to romanticize men, himself or others, as to explain away sin. On the one hand, we should not view men with a cynical eye, seeing them only as meaningless products of chance, but, on the other hand, we should not go to the opposite extreme of seeing them romantically. To do either is to fail to understand who men really are—creatures made in the image of God but fallen.

The Christian understanding of man is not just theoretical. Christians should also be able to show more understanding *to* men than can either the cynic or romantic. We should not be surprised when a man demonstrates he is a sinner because, after all, we know that *all* men are sinners. When someone sits down to talk with me, I should convey to him (even if I do not express it in words) the attitude that he and I are both sinners.

And immediately, when I communicate this perception, a door swings open for dialogue. Nothing will help you as much in meeting people, no matter how far out they are or how caught they are in the modern awfulness, than for them to perceive in you the attitude "we are both sinners." This does not mean that we minimize sin, but we can still exhibit that we understand him because we stand in the same place. We can say "us" rather than just "you." To project "shock" as though we are better slams the door shut. Each of us does not need to look beyond himself to know that men and women are sinners.

Utopianism is terribly cruel because it expects the impossible from people. These expectations are not based

46

on reality. They stand in opposition to the genuine human possibilities afforded by the realism of the Scripture.

Utopianism can cause harm. In the home, in the man-woman relationship, nothing is more cruel than for the wife or husband to build up a false image in his or her mind and then demand that the husband or wife measure up to this false romanticism. Nothing smashes homes more than this. Such behavior is totally contrary to the Bible's doctrine of sin. Even after redemption, we are not perfect in this present life. It is not that we avoid saying sin is sin, but we must have compassion for each other, too.

Utopianism is also harmful in the parent-child relationship. When a parent demands more from his child than the child is capable of giving, the parent destroys him as well as alienates him. But—and this is a special twentieth-century malady—the child can also expect too much of his parents. It cuts both ways. All over the world, perhaps especially in the Western world, children are expecting too much perfection from adults. And because the parent does not measure up to the child's concept of perfection, the child smashes him.

Utopianism is also destructive with a pastor and people. How many pastors have been smashed because their people have expected them to live up to an impossible ideal? And how many congregations have been injured by pastors who forgot that the people in their churches could not be expected to be perfect?

If we demand, in any of our relationships, either perfection or nothing, we will get the nothing. Only when we have learned this will we be Bible-believing Christians, and only then will we understand something of life. Only then can we be more understanding toward men and show real compassion. Consequently, I would repeat, if in any of our relationships of life we demand perfection or nothing, we will have nothing.

A Utopian Self-Concept

Utopianism enters another area to injure Christians, especially serious Christians: A Christian can build up a romantic, idealistic concept of himself and begin expecting absolute perfection from himself. This, too, is a destructive monster.

I am not negating or minimizing sin. But we must understand that the expectation of personal perfection is a romanticism not rooted in Scripture. If I demand perfection from myself, then I will destroy myself. Many Christians vacillate between being permissive in regard to sin toward themselves, on the one hand, and demanding perfection from themselves, on the other. They end up battered and crushed because they do not live up to their own image of perfection.

48 The worst part is that often this image does not have anything to do with biblical standards, with the true law and character of God. A person builds up an image of what a Christian is like as his group or he himself projects it, and then constantly turns inward for subjective analysis and finds he does not measure up to this image. Perhaps the cruelty of utopianism is most manifest at just this point: when an individual applies his own utopianism to himself. "A Christian is like this... ," "A Christian is like that... ," and then he proceeds to an inward destruction. A Christian must understand that sin is sin and yet know that he should not establish for himself a model of "perfection or nothing."

In other words, a Christian can defeat himself in two ways: One is to forget the holiness of God and the fact that sin is sin. The Bible calls us to an ever deeper commitment in giving ourselves to Christ for him to produce his fruit through us. The other is to allow himself to be worn out by Christians who turn Christianity into a romanticism. The realism of the Bible is that God does not excuse sin but neither is he finished with us when he finds sin in us. And for this we should be thankful.

In 1 John we read some wonderful words: "My little children, these things write I unto you, that ye sin not. And if any man sin, we have an advocate with the Father, Jesus Christ the righteous: And he is the propitiation for our sins: and not for ours only, but also for the sins of the whole world" (1 John 2:1-2). Though some people use 1 John to beat themselves into a bloody mass through overly inward inspection, they would not do this if they really understood what John is saying, especially in his preface (1 John 1:1—2:2). For here John makes plain that God does not abandon us when we sin, though sinning is serious and terrible. And that is so whether it was John himself or we Christians living today.

The Christian is called not to sin, and we should say repeatedly to one another: Do not sin. But, if a Christian does sin, he still has an advocate with the Father. Isn't that beautiful? Could you live if it were not true? Not if you really understand sin.

This should make us worship and adore God: Though our call is not to sin, God is not done with us when we do sin. Happily for the apostle John and for Paul, and for us, God is not done with a Christian when a Christian sins. Or God would be finished with all of us.

The Weakness of God's Servants

Among religious writings the Bible is unique in its attitude to its great men. Even many Christian biographies puff up the men they describe. But the Bible exhibits the whole man, so much so that it is almost embarrassing at times. If we would teach our children to read the Bible truly, it would be a good vaccination against cynical realism from the non-Christian side, because the

Bible portrays its characters as honestly as any debunker or modern cynic ever could.

Of course, usually we think about the strong points of the biblical men. And that is all right. Normally, we should look at the victory of biblical characters, the wonder of their closeness to God and the exciting ways God used them according to the faith and faithfulness they displayed. But let us not be embarrassed by the other side—the Bible's candor (even about its greatest leaders), its portrayal of their weaknesses quite without embarrassment and without false show.

Paul wrote to the Romans, "For all have sinned, and come short of the glory of God" (Rom. 3:23)—a simple statement, though stronger in the Greek than it seems in the Authorized Version. The Greek actually says, "All sinned [past] and are coming short [present] of the glory of God." Paul was not saying merely that all men sinned before justification, but that all Christians continue to come short of God's glory. This is the biblical picture even of its own "heroes."

Biblical Examples

If we look through the Scripture even quickly, the weaknesses of God's servants are apparent.

Consider Noah. We should be glad for Noah; he is certainly one of the great men of faith. He was willing to stand alone against his entire culture. No matter where we go in our world, we will not be confronted with conditions so totally adverse. Noah was literally one man against the world.

But this does not keep the Bible from picturing him in his totality. It does not conceal that he once lay drunk and naked in his tent. Some people try to find excuses for Noah. Don't bother, because the Bible does not bother. Just say, Noah was a sinner like you and me, for this is the biblical picture.

The Bible is just as ruthless in speaking about the lies of Abraham, the great father of the faith. At least twice Abraham said that his wife Sarah was his sister. Some critics have foolishly maintained that the instances of deception are really repetitions of one story, but they do not understand what God is communicating. God is stressing that Abraham did not lie only once, but a number of times.

Sarah also told lies. She even tried to lie to God. We may say that she was foolish to try to hide from God the fact that she laughed behind the tent door, but I would say gently to every one of us, including myself, don't we try to lie to God, too?

Isaac imitated his father's lie. Abraham at least told a half-truth when he said Sarah was his sister, for she was the sister by one parent but not the other. Isaac did not have any truth; he just lied.

Jacob cheated his brother. He was a man of the short cut, trying to play all the angles. **51**

Moses lost his temper. The anger which caused him to break the tablets of the law when he saw the golden calf was legitimate (for God shared it), but Moses sinned, on another occasion, by being angry and performing an egotistical act at a most inopportune moment, breaking a picture that God had meant to be given.

Aaron, the priest of God, made an idol, and then to explain its appearance offered one of the silliest explanations one will find anywhere in literature. "I cast in the gold," he said, "and out came this calf." What he had undoubtedly done was to take an engraving tool and deliberately make a mold, or have it made, for the calf. The man who made the idol, the man who made such a foolish excuse, was Aaron, the priest of God.

Miriam became a leper for a time because she complained against God's appointed leadership.

Joshua did not drive the Canaanites out of the promised land as thoroughly as he should have, and hence opened the way for the awful religious compromise that finally destroyed Israel. Gideon did many wonderful things, but then he made an ephod which became a snare to all the people. Samson—we hardly need to mention his licentiousness. David was a "man after God's own heart" and yet an adulterer. He told the most vicious lie one could imagine and planned indirect murder, which in God's sight was real murder.

Solomon, despite all God had given him, at the end of his life became caught in idolatry for the sake of the women he had taken to himself.

Elijah, as great as he was, became trapped in deep despondency after his victory on Mount Carmel. Though we cannot blame him (and here our biblical realism helps us), we must nevertheless call his mood what it was, despondency.

In the New Testament, Peter was a man who had both great strengths and great weaknesses. When he came to Antioch and refused to eat with the Gentile Christians, Paul had to stand against him. Peter, on this side of the resurrection and Pentecost, was, in this specific instance, a man of compromise.

Biblical Principles
This quick look at the weaknesses of some of God's servants makes us aware of a number of biblical principles.

First, all men, even the best of men, need to be saved. This is not just an evangelical cliche. From within the perspective of biblical realism we understand that even if a man is a nice man and shows many evidences of being made in the image of God (and we should be thankful for that), he nevertheless is a sinner who needs to be saved.

The apostle Paul understood Abraham and David as excellent illustrations:

What shall we say then that Abraham our father, as pertaining to the flesh, hath found? For if Abraham were justified by works, he hath whereof to glory; but not before God. For what saith the Scripture? Abraham believed God, and it was counted unto him for righteousness. Now to him that worketh is the reward not reckoned of grace, but of debt. But to him that worketh not, but believeth on him that justifieth the ungodly, his faith is counted for righteousness. Even as David also describeth the blessedness of the man, unto whom God imputeth righteousness without works, Saying, Blessed are they whose iniquities are forgiven, and whose sins are covered. (Rom. 4:1-7)

Both David and Abraham understood that it was not just others, the "they," who needed to be saved but themselves as well.

Second, God reproves sin in all men, even the leaders he appoints. People tend not to do this. It is a fact of life that when a man has tremendous power often nobody reproves him.

But the scriptural perspective is different. There is a real equality among men in the sight of God. Even if a person is a leader of the Lord's people, God will reprove him when he sins.

When Sarah said, "I did not laugh," God said sharply, "Sarah, you did laugh." Because he was angry at the inopportune moment, Moses did not enter the promised land. Aaron watched the pulverized golden calf being scattered on the water and probably had to drink it along with the rest of the people. Miriam became a leper for a time and had to remain outside the camp.

God did not overlook David's sin either. Though the world would have said, "Don't rock the boat," Nathan the prophet, under God's direction, really rocked the boat when he confronted David: "Thou art the man." And Paul, under the leadership of the Holy Spirit, told Peter, "You are wrong" (Gal. 2:11-21).

In Psalm 32, a psalm of repentance, we see God reproving David. After David pours out his heart in love to God, God responds, "I will instruct thee and teach thee in the way which thou shalt go: I will guide thee with mine eye. Be ye not as the horse, or as the mule, which have no understanding: whose mouth must be held in with bit and bridle, lest they come near unto thee" (Ps. 32:8-9). In other words, "David, you're a great leader, and I'll be with you, but don't be like a mule."

The third biblical principle is that the leadership of biblical men was not in every case ended because they sinned. God knew from the beginning who David was. When David was keeping sheep, God had no illusions that here was a perfect man to do God's work. David's sin did not take God by surprise. God is a sovereign God who is never taken by surprise. He knows who men are when he chooses them for leadership. There are no perfect men to do God's work. God is not romantic concerning men.

After these men of faith repented, their leadership continued. John wrote to all Christians (including, surely, those in positions of leadership), "If we confess our sins, he is faithful and just to forgive us our sins, and to cleanse us from all unrighteousness" (1 John 1:9). If we acknowledge we are sinners and do not pretend we are not, and if we confess our sins, then our sins are forgiven. And just as you and I should go on with each other when there has been confession, so God goes on with his people, including his leaders, after their repentance.

Psalm 32 contains an expression of this, and Paul quotes it in Romans 4 when he shows that David under-

54

stood salvation: "Blessed is he whose transgression is forgiven, whose sin is covered. Blessed is the man unto whom the LORD imputeth not iniquity, and in whose spirit there is no guile" (Ps. 32:1-2). David follows this statement with another that forms a unity with it: "When I kept silence, my bones waxed old through my roaring all the day long. For day and night thy hand was heavy upon me: my moisture is turned into the drought of summer" (Ps. 32:3-4). David's silence was a specific kind of silence, a silence of trying to sweep his sins under the table, and during it God's chastening hand was upon him. But when he repented, the hand was lifted:

I acknowledged my sin unto thee, and mine iniquity have I not hid. I said, I will confess my transgressions unto the LORD; and thou forgavest the iniquity of my sin. For this shall everyone that is godly pray unto thee in a time when thou mayest be found: Surely in the floods of great waters they shall not come nigh unto thee. (Ps. 32:5-6)

This is not romanticism; it is cast in terms of sin, chastisement, confession and restoration. It emphasizes what we are pointing out: God dealt with the sins of these leaders, but, after they had confessed, he allowed their leadership to continue.

Attitudes for Leaders

The principles which emerge from the Bible's realistic view of its leaders should affect our attitude toward both those who have been called to lead others and those who have been called to be under another's leadership.

No matter what kind of leadership a Christian is called to—whether a leadership which makes his name great in the Christian world, or the leadership of his own wife and children, or the leadership of a Sunday school class—his *attitude* toward that leadership is the most important thing, not the *size* of his calling.

Some Christians hesitate to take any leadership (whether in affairs large or small) because they are afraid that in the future they will sin. Now if a man intends to sin, that is different. But if he only harbors a fear that someday he will sin, he should remember that God never has a romantic view of anyone he calls to leadership. God knows all men well. And while not minimizing sin or its black results, especially when it is committed by a leader of God's church, we must stress this great comfort: God never looks at any Christian through rose-colored glasses. God calls a person as he is and on the basis of what he can be as he lets Christ produce fruit through him.

What, then, should be a Christian's mentality when he is at some leadership level, whether "high" or "low" and finds sin in his life? The starting place is to be humble and listen. Peter apparently listened to Paul. This does not mean that a person should accept every criticism as justified, but he ought to take time to think and pray over every criticism quietly before the Lord.

Second, a Christian leader must recognize that when he does sin he will be chastened. Christian leadership does not relieve the call to Christian living. God is neither a respecter of persons nor a taker of bribes. All his children are equal. Even if a person is working eighteen hours a day for God, God will chasten him when he sins. So when this happens a leader should not become angry with God. God takes the sin of Christian leaders seriously.

Third, being a Christian leader does not shut him off from the solution to sin described in 1 John and elsewhere in Scripture. Like anybody else, a Christian leader can repent. But there is an added note of urgency. To the extent that we are in a place of leadership (elder, pastor, teacher or whatever), we must especially hurry to repent because, if we do not, not only will we be hurt but so will the Lord's work. If we are in the place of leadership, then hurry—hurry and repent when we sin. In the lives we have examined above, some did not repent quickly, and the Lord's work was spoiled. Saul did not repent at all, and Saul was set aside; his leadership was at an end.

Attitudes for Those Who Are Led

The Bible's realism has implications for followers as well as leaders, and these implications hold true whether we are following men now dead but survived by their books or men now alive. The first rule, which brings us back to where we started, is this: Do not be romantic about your Christian leaders. Do not idolize them. If you do, you will eventually find weaknesses in them, and you will turn on them when you find less than perfection.

Let's say we are studying a biography of Hudson **57** Taylor or William Carey and someone writes of some weakness in him. If we then kick the biography out the window, we are being romantic. We are not understanding the doctrine of sin. We should not be caught between idolizing and despising. If we revere a person too much and then find weaknesses, our first tendency will be to deny any value at all in the man. But this is not right. The Bible is not romantic, and we are not to be romantic either. We are not to minimize sin, but we can expect perfection from no one but God. If from some Christian who has helped us spiritually we demand all or nothing, we will get the nothing.

We can do some things for living Christian leaders that we cannot do for dead ones. For one thing, when a Christian leader confesses sin, he can be restored in love. Sin is sin and the person who sins must be judged. But a repentant leader must be loved.

A good example of judgment followed by forgiveness

occurred in the church at Corinth. In his first letter to the Corinthian Christians, Paul had to write:

It is reported commonly that there is fornication among you, and such fornication as is not so much named among the Gentiles, that one should have his father's wife. And ye are puffed up, and have not rather mourned, that he that hath done this deed might be taken away from among you. For I verily, as absent in body, but present in spirit have judged already, as though I were present, concerning him that hath so done this deed, In the name of our Lord Jesus Christ, when ye are gathered together, and my spirit, with the power of our Lord Jesus Christ, to deliver such an one unto Satan for the destruction of the flesh, that the spirit may be saved in the day of the Lord Jesus. (1 Cor. 5:1-5)

A sin was being flagrantly committed, and, whether or **58** not it was by a leader, it had to be judged.

But we have a caricature of the biblical teaching if we forget the sequel in Paul's second letter to Corinth, written after the judgment had come and the situation had been properly resolved: "Sufficient to such a man is this punishment, which was inflicted of many. So that contrariwise ye ought rather to forgive him, and comfort him, lest perhaps such a one should be swallowed up with overmuch sorrow. Wherefore I beseech you that ye would confirm love toward him" (2 Cor. 2:6-8). Love itself is to be demonstrated toward this person, thus completing the biblical balance. The text says "confirm love toward him," which means much more than "confirm *your* love toward him." Sin must be judged, but as soon as the judgment is received we become sinners if we do not confirm love to the one who has been in sin.

Finally, we must pray for our leaders. In our romanticism we tend to elevate leaders so high that they might as well be sticks of wood. They are no longer people, but symbols. We cannot stand to think of them as sinners. And this is unfair.

Being a leader does not change a man's nature. We must understand our leaders to be men and pray for them as Paul asked the Thessalonians to pray for him: "Finally, brethren, pray for us, that the word of the Lord may have free course, and be glorified" (2 Thess. 3:1). We have an obligation to pray for those who have helped us.

As we reflect the Bible's realism, we will not turn people into sticks of wood and then walk away from them. Rather, we must remember that all Christians *are* men or women, sinners having many victories yet sinners until Jesus comes again. There is no man or woman who does not need prayer. And if a servant of God falls, then the first question I should ask is, "Have I shared his burden?" Specifically, have I treated him as a stick of wood or a religious symbol, or have I prayed for him as a man?　**59**

IV

The
Lord's Work
in the
Lord's Way

For a number of years the theological school from which I graduated sang at its commencement exercises "Give Tongues of Fire." The first verse reads like this:

From ivied walls above the town
The prophet's school is looking down.
And listening to the human din
From marts and streets and homes of men:
As Jesus viewed with yearning deep,
Jerusalem from Olive's steep,
O, crucified and risen Lord,
Give tongues of fire to preach thy Word.

This verse pictures Jesus standing on Olivet, looking over Jerusalem, crying for its lostness. As students go out from studying at Farel House here in Switzerland it is our desire that they will look down over the world, be filled with compassion and speak with tongues of fire into the world's needs.

Because the world is hard, confronting it without God's power is an overwhelming prospect. But tongues of fire are not to be had simply for the asking. The New Testament teaches that certain conditions must exist. In short, they boil down to this: We must do the Lord's work in the Lord's way.

Jesus' Power
Speaking to his disciples and to the church at large, after his resurrection and before his ascension, Jesus said:
All power is given unto me in heaven and in earth. Go ye therefore, and teach all nations, baptizing them in the name of the Father, and of the Son, and of the Holy Ghost: Teaching them to observe all things whatsoever I have commanded you: and, lo, I am with you always, even unto the end of the world. (Mt. 28:18-20)
There is no source of power for God's people—for preaching or teaching or anything else—except Christ himself. Apart from Christ anything which seems to be spiritual power is actually the power of the flesh.

Luke's record of Jesus' pre-ascension statements has exactly the same emphasis: "But ye shall receive power after that the Holy Spirit is come upon you: and ye shall be witnesses unto me both in Jerusalem, and in all Judaea, and in Samaria, and unto the uttermost part of the earth" (Acts 1:8). The force of the Greek is "ye shall receive power; *then* ye shall be witnesses." A specific order is involved: *After* having the Holy Spirit come upon them, the disciples were to witness.

Though we today are immediately indwelt by the Holy Spirit when we accept Christ as Savior, being indwelt is not the same as having the fullness of the power of the Holy Spirit. The disciples had to wait to receive the Spirit at Pentecost. Christians today are to follow the same order: to be indwelt by the Holy Spirit at salvation and to know something of the reality of the power of Christ through the agency of the Holy Spirit—and *then* to work and witness. The order cannot be reversed. There are to be many "fillings."

Doing the Lord's work in the Lord's way is not a matter of being saved and then simply working hard. After Jesus ascended, the disciples waited quietly in prayer for the coming of his Spirit. Their first motion was not toward activism—Christ has risen, now let us be busy. Though they looked at the world with Christ's compassion, they obeyed his clear command to wait before they witnessed. If we who are Christians and therefore indwelt by the Spirit are to preach to our generation with tongues of fire, we also must have something more than an activism which men can easily duplicate. We must know something of the power of the Holy Spirit.

Recognizing Our Need

63

How do we receive something of the power of the Holy Spirit? Though there are great differences between justification and sanctification, we can almost always learn important facets about the latter by considering the former. For example, the story of the Pharisee and the publican who was at the point of conversion is instructive. Before a man is ready to have Christ as his Savior (that is, be justified), he must cry out like the publican (with at least some comprehension of what he is saying), "God, be merciful to me a sinner." A person cannot be a Christian without first recognizing his need of Christ. And as Christians we too must comprehend something of our need for spiritual power. If we think we can operate on our own, if we do not comprehend the need for a power beyond our own, we will never get started. If we think the power of our own cleverness is enough, we will be at a standstill.

Teaching about the Holy Spirit and his indwelling must never be solely a theological concept. Having the proper concept—that we are indwelt by the Holy Spirit when we are saved—we must press on, so that the Spirit's indwelling can bring forth results in our lives. If we want tongues of fire, our first step is not only to stand by, complacently thinking the right theological thoughts. We must have a genuine feeling of need.

Furthermore, this feeling of need is not to be once and for all. A Christian can never say, "I knew the power of the Holy Spirit yesterday, so today I can be at rest." It is one of the existential realities of the Christian life to stand before God consciously recognizing our need.

The publican illustrates that justification requires humbling. Christians must humble themselves to know the sanctifying power of the Holy Spirit. To the extent that we do not humble ourselves, there will be no power of the Holy Spirit in our lives. The Lord's work in the Lord's way is the Lord's work in the power of the Holy Spirit and not in the power of the flesh.

The Central Problem

The *central* problem of our age is not liberalism or modernism, nor the old Roman Catholicism or the new Roman Catholicism, nor the threat of communism, nor even the threat of rationalism and the monolithic consensus which surrounds us. All these are dangerous but not the primary threat. The real problem is this: the church of the Lord Jesus Christ, individually or corporately, tending to do the Lord's work in the power of the flesh rather than of the Spirit. The central problem is always in the midst of the people of God, not in the circumstances surrounding them.

We can sense what this means in practice if we view the statue of Napoleon at the Hotel des Invalides in Paris. As he stands there with his hand in his coat at his breast, he is a personification of I DID THIS. The sculptor has caught the attitude, the attitude of the great man of the world, the one who says in all three tenses, "I did this; I do this; I will do this." This attitude as shown forth so well in the statue personifies "the flesh."

In contrast, we can think of the Lord Jesus himself in the quiet of Gethsemane. As we see there the eternal Son of God who in the incarnation is now also true man and as we hear his words, we perceive no sign of Napoleon's massive egoism. To the contrary, the Lord Jesus said to the Father, "Not my will but thine be done." Unfortunately, we Christians can and often do take Napoleon's stance, but what a contrast to the Lord Jesus himself!

Led by the Spirit
In Matthew 3 is a passage that has often been used as a proof-text for the doctrine of the Trinity: "And Jesus, when he was baptized, went up straightway out of the water: and, lo, the heavens were opened unto him, and he saw the Spirit of God descending like a dove, and lighting upon him: And lo a voice from heaven, saying, 'This is my beloved Son, in whom I am well pleased' " (Mt. 3:16-17).

This is a classical text on the Trinity but it is not to be a bare proof of the Trinity. The passage teaches much more, especially when we place it in the larger context of the next few verses: "Then was Jesus led up of the Spirit into the wilderness to be tempted of the devil" (Mt. 4:1). As soon as Jesus was baptized by the Holy Spirit, he was led by him. If he was thus led by the Holy Spirit, how much more we need so to be! We must not reduce these passages only to a theological statement, even a true theological statement; we must act on them in our lives. Then he goes on to the garden in a few short years and then to die on the cross.

John the Baptist made two prophecies concerning the

Christ. Not only did he say "Behold the Lamb of God, who taketh away the sin of the world" (John 1:29), but he also affirmed, "The same is he which baptizeth with the Holy Ghost" (John 1:33). This second prophecy indicates that not only was Jesus himself baptized and led by the Spirit, but he also baptizes us with the Spirit. Are we, when we accept Christ as our Savior, indwelt by the Holy Spirit? Then we are meant to know something of both his leading and his power.

As we see the Lord Jesus dying on the cross, we who are Bible-believing Christians must fight for the doctrine of the substitutionary atonement. Theological liberalism deliberately destroys the atonement's substitutionary quality, and liberalism controls much of the traditional church structures. So we may have to pay a high price ecclesiastically in order to be faithful to the Bible's teaching. But no matter the cost, let us be faithful. We must stand at all costs for the substitutionary atonement.

The central thrust of the cross *is* the substitutionary atonement, but this does not exhaust its meaning. The cross also teaches a lesson in humility. As Paul wrote to the Philippians, "Let this mind be in you, which was also in Christ Jesus: . . . being found in fashion as a man, he humbled himself, and became obedient unto death, even the death of the cross" (Phil. 2:5, 8). This is where the Christian is to dwell if he is to know something of the power of the Spirit. Just as Christ was humbled in the external space-time world, in the hard stuff of history, not merely in someone's imagination nor in some idealistic setting that makes his death a utopian statement withdrawn from life—so, too, a Christian should have a truly humble heart in the hard reality of the practical world. There is to be a practical reality of the seed falling into the earth to die.

One of the Pope's titles is "servant of servants." And what a tremendous title it is! But in Rome he is carried in a gold-covered chair on the backs of men. I have seen him need help trying to stand because of the weight of the jewels and gold which adorn him. Men had to take his arms and stand him upright. I do not know what is the case today, but in the past when the Pope ate, he ate on a raised platform while other people ate below this servant of servants.

We may react against this, but is it not true that a great deal in our own lives manifests about the same level of humility? We speak of humility and crucifixion, but we are like the Pope, speaking about being a servant of servants and then being carried on the backs of men. While we talk about humility and the power of the Holy Spirit, we spend much of our lives in the stance of Napoleon. As soon as we seek the *Me* rather than follow the example of Christ, we are walking in the flesh rather than in the Spirit.

67

Taking the Lowest Place

Christ taught his disciples that they were not to be called "Rabbi" or "Master" (Mt. 23:8, 10) and that the greatest among them would be the servant of all (Mk. 10:44). Doesn't each one of us tend to reverse this, following our natural inclinations as fallen men while ignoring the Word of God? Don't we like the foremost place? And if this is our mind-set, isn't this living in the flesh, and to that extent leaving the Spirit no place?

Seeking the highest place is in direct contradiction to the teaching of the Lord. Christ instructed his disciples, "But when thou art bidden [to a wedding feast], go and sit down in the lowest room" (Lk. 14:10). If we are going to do the Lord's work in the Lord's way, we must take Jesus' teaching seriously: He does not want us to press on to the greatest place unless he himself makes it impossible to do otherwise. Taking the lower place in a practical way (thus reflecting the mentality of Christ who humbled himself even to death on a cross) should be a Christian's choice.

Even if we have an "office," like a parent with a child or an elder in a church, it is only the office that sets us apart. We are not greater than those over whom we have authority. If we have the world's mentality of wanting the foremost place, we are not qualified for Christian leadership. This mentality can lift us into ecclesiastical leadership or fit us for being a big name among men, but it unfits us for real spiritual leadership.

To the extent that we want power we are in the flesh, and the Holy Spirit has no part in us. Christ put a towel around himself and washed his disciples' feet (John 13: 4-14). We should ask ourselves from time to time, "Whose feet am I washing?" Some churches have made foot-washing into a third sacrament; members wash each other's feet during their worship service. While most of us think it is a mistake to make this a sacrament, let us admit: It is ten thousand times better to wash each other's feet in a literal way than never to wash anybody's feet in any way. It would be far better for us to make a mistake and institute a third sacrament of literal foot-washing than to live out our lives without once consciously choosing to serve each other. Doing the Lord's work in the Lord's way is not some exotic thing; it is having and practicing the mentality which Christ commands.

Seeking God's Approval

In addition to teaching us not to seek power, the Lord Jesus taught us not to seek human praise. Those who seek the praise of men, he said, have their reward when they have the praise. We often read this pietistically and miss the point. Jesus meant what he said: If our aim has been praise and power and we have it, either in the world or in the church, we have had it. It is the one who does not seek it now who will have the praise when he stands before the dear Lord's face. Scripture is clear that we must either humble ourselves now or be humbled in the future.

In 1 Corinthians, Paul pictures a "believers' judgment," when every Christian will stand not for salvation (that is determined at the cross when the individual accepts Christ as Savior) but to have his works as a Christian tried. No Christian will lose his salvation in this judgment, but whatever he has done for himself (including seeking power and the praise of men) will be lost. If he has not humbled himself in this life, he will be humbled then. There is no third way.

Trusting God's Methods

Is it not amazing: Though we know the power of the Holy Spirit can be ours, we still ape the world's wisdom, trust its forms of publicity, its noise, and imitate its ways of manipulating men! If we try to influence the world by using its methods, we are doing the Lord's work in the flesh. If we put activity, even good activity, at the center rather than trusting God, then there may be the power of the world but we will lack the power of the Holy Spirit.

The key question is this: As we work for God in this fallen world, what are we trusting in? To trust in particular methods is to copy the world and to remove ourselves from the tremendous promise that we have something different—the power of the Holy Spirit rather than the power of human technique.

Under the leadership of Moses and Joshua, the Jews marched when the ark marched and they stood still when the ark stood still. They did not rush ahead if God did not order the ark (which represented himself) to be moved. Sometimes they stayed in one place for long periods. We Christians, individually and corporately, must learn to wait like this. Tongues of fire are not for us if we are so busy doing the clever thing that we never wait quietly to find out whether the ark of the Lord has gone ahead or stayed. Once after I had given a message like this, a man told me, "You have opened a door for me. What you say is true. I am on many Christian boards, and I have large holdings in cotton mills. So I am in one kind of business meeting at one time and another kind of business meeting at another. And sometimes in the midst of a meeting I will suddenly look up and say, Which meeting am I in?" He could see no difference whatsoever; in both cases just the clever thing was being done. This is not the way to have spiritual power. The Lord's work must be done in the Lord's way.

The Battle in the Heavenlies

70 The real battle is not fought by Christians just against forces in this world, whether theological, cultural or moral. The real battle is in the heavenlies. The Scripture, therefore, insists that we cannot win our portion of the engagement with earthly weapons.

Paul's letter to the Ephesians contains the classic expression:

Finally, my brethren, be strong in the Lord, and in the power of his might. Put on the whole armour of God, that ye may be able to stand against the wiles of the devil. For we wrestle not against flesh and blood, but against principalities, against powers, against the rulers of the darkness of this world, against the spiritual hosts of wickedness in the heavenly places. Wherefore, take unto you the whole armour of God, that ye may be able to withstand in the evil day, and having done all, to stand. Stand, therefore, having your loins girt about with truth, having on the breastplate of righteousness; and your feet shod with the preparation of the gospel of peace; Above all, taking the shield of faith, wherewith ye shall be able to quench all the fiery darts of the wicked one. And take the helmet of salvation, and the sword of the Spirit, which is the word of God: Praying always with all prayer and supplication in the Spirit, and watching thereunto with all perseverance and supplication for all saints. (Eph. 6:10-18)

There is nothing in this list that the world accepts as a way of working, but there are no other ways to fight the spiritual battle. Imagine the devil or a demon entering your room right now. You have a sword by your side, so when you see him you rush at him and stab him. But the sword passes straight through and doesn't faze him! The most awesome modern weapon you could think of could not destroy him. Whenever we do the Lord's work in the flesh, our strokes "pass right through" because we do not battle earthly forces; the battle is spiritual and requires spiritual weapons.

Besides, if we fight the world with copies of its own weapons, we will fail, because the devil will honor these with his own, but our Lord will not honor these with us, for that does not give him the glory. They may bring some results—activism does have its results—but they will not be the ones the Lord wants. Our hands will be empty of honor from God because he will not be getting the glory. We must not try to serve the Lord with our own kind of humanism and egoism.

In this war if Christians win a battle by using worldly means, they have really lost. On the other hand, when we seem to lose a battle while waiting on God, in reality we have won. The world may mistakenly say, "They have lost." But if God's people seem to be beaten in a specific battle not because of sin or lack of commitment or lack of prayer or lack of paying a price but because they have waited on God and refused to resort to the flesh, then they have won.

Getting Things Done

Let us not think that waiting on the Lord will mean getting less done. The truth is that by doing the Lord's work in the Lord's way we will accomplish more, not less. You need not fear that if you wait for God's Spirit you will not get as much done as if you charge ahead in the flesh. After all, who can do the most, you or the God of heaven and earth?

Nor should we think that our role will be passive. The moving of the Holy Spirit should not be contrasted with either proper self-fulfillment or tiredness. To the contrary, both the Scriptures and the history of the church teach that if the Holy Spirit is working, the whole man will be involved and there will be much cost to the Christian. The more the Holy Spirit works, the more Christians will be used in battle, and the more they are used, the more there will be personal cost and tiredness. It is quite the opposite of what we might first think. People often cry out for the work of the Holy Spirit and yet forget that when the Holy Spirit works, there is always tremendous cost to the people of God—weariness and tears and battles.

The Lord brings the real contrast into focus in Galatians: "This I say then, Walk in the Spirit, and ye shall not fulfill the lust of the flesh. . . . If we live in the Spirit, let us also walk in the Spirit. Let us not be desirous of vain glory, provoking one another, envying one another" (Gal. 5:16, 25-26). In these verses, walking in the Spirit (that is, doing the Lord's work in the Lord's way) is not contrasted with tiredness and cost but with vain glory. We cannot have God's power and deliberately place the *Me* in the center of our lives. We cannot know much about walking in the Spirit until we realize and implement the washing of feet and the humility of the cross. As long as vain glory exists, it will have destructive results, such as "provoking one another, envying one another."

If we do not want to waste our lives after we have become Christians, then we must understand the importance of having a humble, quiet heart and the power of the Holy Spirit. While we were working in Champery, one of the people who accepted Christ as Savior was an elderly woman of the German aristocracy. She was a dear woman whom we came to love very much. After she had accepted the Lord, she said that her one regret was that most of her life had been completely wasted. The high social life of Egypt, in which she had lived for many years, and similar circles in which she had traveled in various parts of the world had been without meaning. It is not only non-Christians, however, who can lose years. Christians must also be careful not to throw away large portions of their lives.   73

Practicing the Biblical Position

Humanism presses in upon us, constantly challenging our very lifestyle. So we must not fail to practice its opposite—the biblical position—presenting a real, practical contrast in our day-to-day living. Is not the central problem of our generation that the world looks upon the church and sees it trying to do the Lord's work in the flesh? Let us ask ourselves the hard questions: Do we really believe God exists, and do we really believe God?

Often men have acted as though one has to choose between reformation and revival. Some call for reformation, others for revival, and they tend to look at each other with suspicion. But reformation and revival do not stand in contrast to one another; in fact, both words are related to the concept of restoration. Reformation speaks of a restoration to pure doctrine, revival of a restoration in the Christian's life. Reformation speaks of a return to the teachings of Scripture, revival of a life brought into proper relationship to the Holy Spirit. The great moments in church history have come when these two restorations have occurred simultaneously. There cannot be true revival unless there has been reformation, and reformation is not complete without revival. May we be those who know the reality of both reformation and revival, so that this poor dark world in which we live may have an exhibition of a portion of the church returned to both pure doctrine and a Spirit-filled life.

As I see it, the Christian life must be comprised of three concentric circles, each of which must be kept in its proper place. In the outer circle must be the correct theological position, true biblical orthodoxy and the purity of the visible church. This is first, but if that is all there is, it is just one more seedbed for spiritual pride. In the second circle must be good intellectual training and comprehension of our own generation. But having only this leads to intellectualism and again provides a seedbed for pride. In the inner circle must be the humble heart—the love of God, the devotional attitude toward God. There must be the daily *practice* of the reality of the God whom we know is there. These three circles must be properly established, emphasized and related to each other. At the center must be kept a living relationship to the God we know exists. When each of these three circles is established in its proper place, there will be tongues of fire and the power of the Holy Spirit. Then, at the end of my life, when I look back over my work since I have been a Christian, I will see that I have not wasted my life. The Lord's work will be done in the Lord's way.

The last verse of "Give Tongues of Fire" summarizes it so well:

O Son of man, O Son of God!
Whose love bought all men by his blood,

74

> Give us thy mind, thy soul's desire,
> Thy heart of love, Thy tongue of fire
> That we thy gospel may proclaim
> To every man in thy great name!
> O crucified and risen Lord,
> Give tongues of fire to preach thy Word.

This should be the desire of our hearts. But if we are going to know it rather than just sing it and talk it, we must not do the Lord's work in the flesh. We must do the *Lord's* work in the *Lord's* way.

V

Walking through the Mud

It is difficult for a Christian to walk through the mud without getting dirty. The mud I am speaking of is the dirt of the world. The apostle Paul commanded, "And be not conformed to this world: but be ye transformed by the renewing of your mind, that ye may prove what is that good, and acceptable, and perfect, will of God" (Rom. 12:2).

There is a world spirit which has existed ever since man revolted against God. We may call it some technical name such as humanism or rationalism, or simply the spirit of the world. It is the spirit of anti-law, and anti-law of a very special kind, anti-law in revolution against God himself. It is characterized by man putting himself at the center of everything, making himself the standard of value. This is why we call this spirit of revolution against God *humanism*. It is Man with a capital *M*. It is man saying, "I will only accept knowledge that I myself can generate out from myself." This is why we relate this spirit of revolution against God to the word *rationalism*. For any individual, whether he is a philosopher or a simple person, this rebellion is never an abstraction. It is not just Man putting man in the center of everything, but it is an individual putting *Me* at the center of everything. There is diversity in the unity of the world spirit: Each age manifests the spirit in its own way. The basic attitude is always the same, but its particular manifestation in each generation must be sought out. If we are to resist being dirtied by the spirit of the world, we must not only reject its essential characteristic but also search out and resist the special form it is taking in our own generation.

When Paul came into Europe, he faced a civilization built on the false religion of his day. We are naive if we do not realize that we too are surrounded by a uniform culture (I sometimes call it a monolithic culture), which claws at us from our birth to our death. Not only in obvious ways we can easily comprehend but also in subtle ways, a thousand voices express its mentality. Yet when we translate what we hear, we discover that there is really only one voice, the spirit of the world, and the particular form that world spirit takes in our day.

The World Spirit Today
What form does the world spirit take today? We could answer in terms of philosophy, by saying that men have given up the hope of absolutes and universals and placed their confidence in synthesis. Or we could say that men today live their lives in a dichotomy, a split world of thinking. They separate reason from values and meaning and purpose.

We could answer in terms of art. As a statement of humanistic philosophy going back to the Renaissance we might imagine Michelangelo's great rebellious figures tearing themselves out of hunks of marble, tearing themselves loose from everything else, to stand alone as man. But in our day man's self-concept has diminished. The message of modern art is that everything (including truth) is in flux. Op art tells us we cannot trust our eyes, while pop art tells us that all that is important is the experience of the moment.

We could answer in terms of music and mention John Cage's contention that since everything is produced by chance, music also must be composed by chance. In some modern dance, too, individual significance is crushed out because everything exists by chance.

The contemporary form of the world spirit in modern theology teaches that there is no normative scripture and therefore no absolutes. This theology has left religion no better than Goethe's cross with roses, an emotional uplift.

But the main point is this: Being conformed to the world spirit does not refer merely to outward acts; the real battle is in our thought world. Resisting in our thought life is essential. Whether we are conformed externally will always depend on whether we have or have not conformed internally to the spirit of the world. The battle is of the mind. "Be ye transformed by the renewing of your mind," Paul admonished.

If I am not going to be dirtied as I walk through the mud of the world, the first thing I must do, by God's grace, is not to be conformed to the present form of the world spirit in the world of my thoughts.

The World Spirit in Morals

We who are Bible-believing Christians respond: We are not conformed in the areas of philosophy and theology. Good! But let us go on.

Once I understand God's truth, I must put it into action. True Bible-believing Christians not only affirm the authority of Scripture but also live on biblical principles. Christians must affirm the doctrines of Scripture and they must apply them. If we use as a smoke screen the fact that we are not conformed to the philosophy and theology of our day, thinking that then we are automatically free from the world's contamination, we still are not really Bible-believing Christians.

It is especially easy to become contaminated in the area of morals. Today's world does not just have *false* moral standards—it has *no* moral standards in any absolute sense. We think immediately of sexual morals, but it is not just sexual morals. It is all morals in private and public life. Modern men, in the absence of absolutes, have polluted all aspects of morality, making standards completely hedonistic and relativistic. The world has dressed these up in its own vocabulary and called it situational ethics. Every situation is judged subjectively with no absolute to which to appeal.

Young people today (especially, let us say, much of the hippie generation) have sensed this and have brought forth an idealism which is tied to the rejection of the hypocrisy of the previous generation's morals. But the dilemma, of course, is that these utopians have no standards either. So instead of finding what they hope for, they are led into fresh sorrows.

We can remember Vincent van Gogh, who tried to fulfill his idealism by starting a community in southern France. He was desperately in search of something beautiful. Yet as we study his self-portraits, we see them disintegrate year after year, till at the end of his life they are less than human. As we look at the hippie world, we can see the same thing—beginning with an idealism it ends destroyed. We must cry for our present world, because the idealists who have screamed so loudly against the falseness and hypocrisy of the plastic culture have ended up in an even worse position—the inhumanity and the destruction of everything they hoped to accomplish.

What Does the Scripture Teach?

Because we live in a day of moral relativity, our need to know what the Scripture says about moral absolutes is all the greater. What does the Scripture teach? First, consider Jesus' answer to the prime question: "Master, which is the great commandment in the law?" Jesus responded, "Thou shalt love the Lord thy God with all thy heart, and with all thy soul, and with all thy mind. This is the first and great commandment" (Mt. 22:36-38).

It is sad that a person can hear this and not hear it, for some theologians use precisely this command as an excuse for believing nothing and holding no absolute moral standards. We can understand these verses accurately and specifically only in the context of the entire Scripture. Jesus' reply was not meant to be evasive. Rather, it summarized the first table of the law:

And God spake all these words, saying, I am the LORD thy God, which have brought thee out of the land of Egypt, out of the house of bondage. Thou shalt have no other gods before me. Thou shalt not make unto thee any graven image, or any likeness of anything that is in heaven above, or that is in the earth beneath, or that is in the water under the earth. Thou shalt not bow down thyself to them, nor serve them: for I the LORD thy God am a jealous God, visiting the iniquity of the fathers upon the children unto the third and fourth generation of them that hate me; And shewing mercy unto thousands of them that love me, and keep my commandments. Thou shalt not take the name of the LORD thy God in vain; for the LORD will not hold him guiltless that taketh his name in vain. Remember the sabbath day, to keep it holy. Six days shalt thou labour, and do all thy work: But the seventh day is the sabbath of the LORD thy God: in it thou shalt not do any work, thou, nor thy son, nor thy daughter, thy manservant, nor thy maidservant, nor thy cattle, nor thy stranger that is within thy gates: For in six days the LORD made heaven and earth, the sea, and all that in them is, and rested the seventh day: wherefore the LORD blessed the sabbath day, and hallowed it. (Ex. 20:1-11)

These verses tell us what Jesus meant when he said, "Thou shalt love the Lord thy God with all thy heart, and with all thy soul, and with all thy mind." He was not making a vague, relativistic, twentieth-century religious statement. Rather, he was affirming that these commandments are God's standards and that he does not expect believers to be conformed to any thinking that would chisel them down.

Jesus, of course, added a second commandment—"Thou shalt love thy neighbor as thyself" (Mt. 22:39)—which men make even more vague and situational. They excuse everything under the word *love*. But God's law is not relativistic. The remainder of the Decalogue gives this command definite content:

Honour thy father and thy mother: that thy days may be long upon the land which the LORD thy God giveth thee. Thou shalt not murder. Thou shalt not commit adultery. Thou shalt not steal. Thou shalt not bear false witness against thy neighbour. Thou shalt not covet thy neighbour's house, thou shall not covet thy neighbour's wife, nor his manservant, nor his maidservant, nor his ox, nor his ass, nor any thing that is thy neighbour's. (Ex. 20:12-17)

These commandments define what it means to love my neighbor as myself. They are never allowed to be anything less than absolute and down to earth.

Some people try to escape their force by limiting the definition of *neighbor*. But when Jesus was asked "Who is my neighbor?" he told the parable of the good Samaritan, which teaches that every person we meet is our *neighbor* (Lk. 10:29-37). No man anywhere, no matter who he is or what he is like, no matter what language he speaks, what skin color he has, or what social or cultural group he belongs to, is excluded from being my *neighbor.* This is an absolute standard, which we must practice, not just a vague emotional reaction. If we do not practice this, we are sinning and will be judged.

In the Sermon on the Mount, Jesus goes even further:

But I say unto you, love your enemies, bless them that curse you, do good to them that hate you, and pray for them which despitefully use you, and persecute you; That ye may be the children of your Father which is in heaven: for he maketh his sun to rise on the evil and on the good, and sendeth rain on the just and on the unjust. (Mt. 6:44-45)

Jesus did not simply define *neighbor* as *friend,* our group or someone who treats us nicely. We are to love the man who does something mean and nasty to us, the man who deliberately sabotages us. This is God's absolute standard: We are never to steal, bear false witness, commit adultery or covet, regardless of the persons we are dealing with. He is speaking here about any man we meet anywhere in the world. God allows no relativism in any of this, none whatsoever.

Yielded to Righteousness

After he is converted, a Christian has moral choices to make, existentially, moment by moment. He must continually choose to yield himself to God:

Let not sin therefore reign in your mortal body, that ye should obey it in the lusts thereof. Neither yield ye your members as instruments of unrighteousness unto sin: but yield yourselves unto God, as those that are alive from the dead, and your members as instruments of righteousness unto God. For sin shall not have dominion over you: for ye are not under the law, but under grace. What then? Shall we sin, because we are not under the law, but under grace? God forbid. Know ye not, that to whom ye yield yourselves servants to obey, his servants ye are to whom ye obey; whether of sin unto death, or obedience unto righteousness? (Rom. 6:12-16)

For Christians, surrounded by the spirit of the world, the Word of God says there is a practical morality based on absolutes. We are not to use these absolutes only as theoretical tools when we argue against a relativist. We are, by the grace of God, to *practice* them, to *live* them, to yield ourselves to righteousness. We are to live in practice upon the basis which God has revealed to us as the expression of his character. Using this to win arguments without living upon them is a special kind of horribleness.

Many Bible passages reveal God's absolutes for dealing with other people and with the problems of life. In Ephesians, for instance, Paul makes a general statement and then gives three practical couplets:

Submitting yourselves one to another in the fear of God. *Wives*, submit yourselves unto your own husbands, as unto the Lord. Therefore as the church is subject unto Christ, so let the wives be to their own husbands in everything. *Husbands*, love your wives, even as Christ also loved the church, and gave himself for it. *Children*, obey your parents in the Lord: for this is right. And, ye *fathers*, provoke not your children to wrath: but bring them up in the nurture and admonition of the Lord. *Servants*, be obedient to them that are your masters according to the flesh, with fear and trembling, in singleness of your heart, as unto Christ. And ye *masters*, do the same things unto them, forbearing threatening: knowing that your Master also is in heaven; neither is there respect of persons with him. (Eph. 5:21-22, 24-25; 6:1, 4-5, 9)

In each instance, the first command means nothing unless seen in balance with the second part of the couplet. Couplet one is wives-husbands. Couplet two is children-fathers. Couplet three is servants-masters. The twentieth-century translation I would give concerning fathers is, "Fathers, do not drive your children up the wall!" The practice of each portion of each couplet is a rule for a Christian's life.

The section of the Bible which perhaps best portrays the tension between the spirit of the world and the spirit of Christ is in Galatians 5. First, Paul describes the world spirit:

> Now the works of the flesh are manifest, which are these; Adultery, fornication, uncleanness, lasciviousness, idolatry, witchcraft, hatred, variance, emulations, wrath, strife, seditions, heresies, envyings, murders, drunkenness, revellings, and such like: of the which I tell you before, as I have also told you in the past, that they which do such things shall not inherit the kingdom of God. (Gal. 5:19-21)

In contrast, Paul portrays the fruit of the Holy Spirit:

> But the fruit of the Spirit is love, joy, peace, longsuffering, gentleness, goodness, faith, meekness, temperance: against such there is no law. And they that are Christ's have crucified the flesh with the affections and lusts. If we live in the Spirit, let us also walk in the Spirit. (Gal. 5:22-25)

God's desire for one who is a Christian and thus indwelt by the Holy Spirit is to maintain these standards and to present a contrast to the spirit of the world. We cannot do it by ourselves; we must walk in the Spirit and look to Christ to bear his fruit through us.

Being a Bible-believing Christian will be little more than a flag we wave, unless we live out the Bible's moral principles. Struggling against modern theology is important; so, too, is fighting for the purity of the visible church. But unless we are conformed to the standards of the Word of God rather than to the world, espousing proper doctrine is merely flag-waving.

The World Spirit in Entertainment

We have been speaking of morals as one area where the world spirit manifests itself. Another area is entertainment in order to forget. A sociologist has recently written that as computers and machines take over more and more tasks, people will have to stop being achievement-centered. Many are saying that in the next generation, the government's chief job will be to devise ways of keeping a growing mass of people entertained, because machines will have taken their jobs.

"That will be a horrible day," we say. But in a different way it is already upon us. People today are afraid to be alone. This fear is a dominant mark of our society. Many now ceaselessly sit in the cinema or read novels about other people's lives or watch dramas. Why? Simply to avoid facing their own existence. Many of us can sit in front of the television and, except on rare occasions, not face our own private life. Entertainment so fills every cranny of our culture we can easily escape thinking.

Alcohol has always been a way of escape; now our generation has added drugs. And many young people are now leaving drugs only to return to alcohol. But alcoholics and drug users are not the only escapists. So is the one who stands with a transistor radio plugged into his ear much of the day. No one seems to want (and no one can find) a place for quiet—because, when you are quiet, you have to face reality. But many in the present generation dare not do this because on their own basis reality leads them to meaninglessness; so they fill their lives with entertainment, even if it is only noise.

Some friends once gave a birthday dinner for my wife

and me at Villars. We sat in the sun, looking out across tremendous mountains, and we had time to think. But nobody could think because over a loudspeaker a radio program was blaring out; a man was shouting something that nobody could understand. Nevertheless, when I asked the management to turn it off, they said everybody else wanted it on. The twentieth-century entertainment and noise follow us everywhere.

People also escape in the high-speed vacations we have developed. When our family first came to Europe in 1948, we lived in La Rosiaz, above Lausanne. At that time it was a favorite place for families to begin hikes. Looking out the window during vacation times and on Sunday afternoons, we saw walking past our home dozens of families with rucksacks—walking together in quietness.

Almost nobody does this now. Today people in droves hurry up past Huemoz to Villars on the road to get to the ski hills so they can rush down them as fast as they can so they can hurry up again in order to rush down again. In a way this is funny, but in a way we must cry, for it is a part of the spirit of our age which Paul tells us to resist. The Christian is supposed to be the very opposite: There is a place for proper entertainment, but we are not to be caught up in ceaseless motion which prevents us from ever being quiet. Rather we are to put everything second so we can be alive to the voice of God and allow it to speak to us and confront us.

So when Paul says, "Be not conformed to this world: but be ye transformed by the renewing of your mind, that ye may prove what is that good, and acceptable, and perfect, will of God," he is not talking only about philosophical and theological beliefs. He is talking about resisting the pressure to conform to false moral standards and the escapism of a mad busyness which are even harder to wrestle with than philosophical and theological dangers. As Christians, we must follow God's absolute moral standards, and we must not be robbed of a place of quietness with God.

Facing Reality

Even with the pressures of the world spirit upon him, a Christian can face reality. Writing to the Ephesians, Paul makes a striking contrast: "And be not drunk with wine, wherein is excess; but be filled with the Spirit; speaking to yourselves in psalms and hymns and spiritual songs, singing and making melody in your heart to the Lord" (Eph. 5:18-19).

Young people today have quite properly asked, "Why shouldn't I escape through drugs when my father and mother and aunts and uncles escape through alcohol? What's the difference?" There is no difference. The person who escapes in alcohol and then acts shocked when his child uses drugs is being unreasonable.

But a Christian is not supposed to need an escape—alcohol, drugs, constant noise and entertainment or whatever. Not that we do not sometimes take the easy route. We do, for none of us is perfect. But this is not the standard we are pressing toward. Both in theory and practice Christians can dare to face the realities of life unclouded. We do not need these things to fill the crannies of our lives. In fact, we should want to face reality: the glory of the world God has created and the wonder of being human—yes, and even the awful reality of the Fall and the tragedy of marred men and women, even our own flawed character. We are not to be people of escape. The Christian is to be the realist. To face reality as born again and indwelt by the Holy Spirit is the Christian's calling.

Since God's truth always has a corporate as well as an individual application, we can also say that a local congregation is wrong if it constantly seeks diversion and activity. Some entertainment and activity is appropriate, but as we look at the church, even much of the evangelical church, what we see is tragic, for the church is using entertainment or just plain busyness to attract non-Christians. This is a poverty. But it is an even greater poverty if we need these to hold Christians after they are Christians. May God have mercy on us if this is so. For we are doing Christians a terrible disservice; we are enabling them to avoid facing the world and each other. This too is a way of being drunk. And surely some of evangelicalism is being infused with this generation's relativity in morals. Consider the growing acceptance by evangelical churches of divorce for non-biblical reasons, rather than living under God's commands concerning this.

True Compassion

Returning to Paul's command in Romans 12 to be transformed rather than conformed, we can see that it is neither trite nor pietistic in the bad sense. It should be a reality in both our thinking and acting. *Not being conformed to the world spirit in philosophy and theology does not give us a right to be conformed in these other things.* To the extent that I am not conformed to the teaching of the Bible, the Word of God in my life, I am entrapped in the mire of the world. To the extent that I am not living on Bible principles, I am walking through mud and getting dirty. The same thing is true of the Christian congregation or Christian group. We must call sin sin, and resist it, not just explain it away psychologically.

We say we must have compassion for the lost world and not be too harsh. This is true: We must show love and sympathy. But if I have compassion, if I want to show love to the world, I individually, and we in our groups, must obey God's commands. When I am conformed to the world's sin, not only do I offend God with that sin, but I diminish the drawing power of the gospel. Jesus said,

Ye are the salt of the earth: but if the salt have lost its savour, wherewith shall it be salted? It is thenceforth good for nothing, but to be cast out and to be trodden under foot of men. Ye are the light of the world. A city that is set on an hill cannot be hid. Neither do men light a candle, and put it under a bushel, but on a candlestick; and it giveth light unto all that are in the house. Even so let your light shine before men, that they may see your good works, and glorify your Father which is in heaven. (Mt. 5:13-16)

Christians must not let the world defile them. If the world sees us conforming to its standards and its relativism, it will not listen to what we say. It will have no reason to.

The world is turning to false answers on every side, and we say we wish to reach people with the truth. Some people are honestly looking for real, fundamental answers, seeking truth in the confusion of our generation. But if they look at Christians who emphasize that the Bible is truth and they see a lack of absolutes in our thinking and acting (both individually and corporately), or if all they see is another form of escapism couched in either secular or religious words, who can blame them if they turn away?

VI

Joseph

This sermon could be considered three short sermons, for the Bible's emphasis on Joseph gives three lessons, one involving Joseph and Christ, another Joseph and David, and a third Joseph in adversity.

First, let us survey Joseph's history. Joseph was the eleventh son of Jacob. He was born to the beloved Rachel, who had only two children, and thus he was especially loved by his father. As a mark of love for Joseph, Jacob gave him a coat. Traditionally, the Authorized Version's translation "a coat of many colors" has been accepted, but it is hard to tell from the Hebrew exactly what the coat's distinctive feature was. But that does not matter. What matters is that the coat showed Jacob's special love for Joseph.

The boy had a special character, too. When his brothers did things that were wrong, Joseph talked to his father about it rather than going along with them. From the biblical emphasis, it is quite plain that this was not simply tale-bearing, which is nothing to praise. Rather, it was a demonstration of the young Joseph's character. But by doing this Joseph earned his brothers' ill will. First they envied him, then they hated him.

As time went on, Joseph had dreams, not ordinary dreams but dreams from God that marked him as one whom God was going to use. The first dream was of sheaves in a field. "My sheaf stood upright," he told his brothers, "and, behold, your sheaves stood round about, and made obeisance to my sheaf" (Gen. 37:7). Later, God gave an even more striking dream, in which the sun, moon and eleven stars bowed before Joseph. The Bible makes clear that these represented Joseph's father, his brothers and whoever had been serving as the mother of the home since Joseph's own mother had died.

94 When he was still a boy during his seventeenth year, his older brothers had the flocks a long way from home. Because Jacob had no mail service, telephone, or walkie-talkie, he had difficulty knowing what was happening to his sons when they were away many days. So he called Joseph and gave him the difficult assignment of making contact with the brothers, difficult and dangerous because it required traveling a long distance, probably on foot. Joseph's response to Jacob's order is significant. Without discussion, the boy said, "Here am I," which simply means, "I'll do what you say." And he started out to walk to Shechem.

Shechem was a long distance, fifty miles one way, and, when he got there, he found to his disappointment that his brothers had moved on still farther. He finally found them in Dothan, fifteen miles beyond Shechem, which made his walk a total of sixty-five miles. He must have been pleased as he came over the Judean hills and saw the great mob of sheep. But his brothers were not pleased. As soon as they saw him, even before he arrived, they made plans to kill him. They moved from their first two steps of envy and hate to the final step of murder.

As they planned the murder, however, Reuben, the oldest brother, made a counter suggestion: that they put Joseph into a pit. This probably showed some element of kindness, though it is difficult to know for sure. A painter or poet would find the scene challenging, and a dramatist would find this an especially apt subject. For his brothers put him into a pit, and then, the text says, "they sat down to eat bread" (Gen. 37:25). The younger brother in the pit, the older brothers eating bread and enjoying themselves—a scene of high drama of the cruelty of man to man.

Some Ishmaelite traders came along soon after, and the brothers sold them the boy for twenty pieces of silver. The Bible does not tell us Joseph's emotional response, but one gets the sense that these were real historic characters not just cardboard men. 95

Whether Joseph pleaded or not, his brothers sent him away as a slave, probably bound with a rope around his neck, walking behind a camel away from his home and, it would seem, away from all hope. Then his brothers took his splendid coat and dipped it in animal blood in order to convince Jacob that a wild beast had devoured his favorite son.

Joseph in Egypt
Down in Egypt, Joseph was sold as a slave into the house of Potiphar, a great man in Egypt, the captain of the guard. In Potiphar's household Potiphar saw that everything Joseph did prospered, whether in the house or in the field. So Joseph gradually came to a place of leadership second only to Potiphar. Then we are told Potiphar's wife "cast her eyes upon Joseph" (Gen. 39:7). Because he refused to lie with her, she lied about him to

Potiphar, who cast him into prison. So far the path has been constantly downward—sold, made a slave and now imprisoned. However, gradually he came to a place of leadership there, too, and the prison keeper eventually committed all the prisoners to Joseph and "looked not to anything that was under his hand" (Gen. 39:23). At that point in history, Pharaoh threw both his chief butler and chief baker into prison for doing something which displeased him. They each dreamed a dream which Joseph interpreted: Pharaoh would kill the baker but release the butler.

Two full years later, Pharaoh also had a dream, and the butler remembered the imprisoned Hebrew who could interpret dreams. We do not know the butler's motivation, but we do know he brought Joseph to Pharaoh. After Joseph interpreted Pharaoh's dream, we find Joseph saying, "It is not in me. God has shown Pharaoh something in the dream. God has shown you what he is about to do" (Gen. 41:16, 25). Because Joseph successfully interpreted the dream, Pharaoh made him leader of all the land of Egypt. Pharaoh held the ultimate power, the throne, but under him Joseph was leader of the land.

Joseph was then thirty years old. He had had thirteen long years of learning God's lessons before he did anything that seems important. Now he controlled the economic life of Egypt, which, because Egypt was a great economic center, meant he had power over much of the known world. When his first child was born, Joseph called him *Manasseh*, which means *forgetting*. He said, "I'm calling him Manasseh because God has made me forget all my toil" (Gen. 41:51).

The event God had revealed to Pharaoh in the dream was a coming famine. So Joseph's main task was to store up food. The famine became international, covering all that portion of the world, which meant that people from other countries flocked to Egypt to get the food Joseph had been wise enough to store. Among these people were ten of Joseph's brothers. After he tested them, Joseph revealed who he was to them. Then with five more years of famine to come he brought Jacob and his household (a total of seventy people—all the Jews in the world at that time) down to safety in Egypt, where they settled in the land of Goshen. When Jacob died, the Egyptians mourned for a long period—not for Jacob's sake but for Joseph's, because Joseph was a great man in the land. Jacob was embalmed, the only Jew we know of whose body went through the long Egyptian embalming process.

Joseph himself died when he was 110 years old. In faith, he instructed his children not to leave his bones in Egypt (Gen. 50:24-25). As Hebrews puts it, "By faith Joseph, when he died, made mention of the departing of the children of Israel; and gave commandment concerning his bones" (Heb. 11:22). He knew that God had made a promise and, being a man of God, he knew that God would fulfill it. With this admonition to his children, Joseph's story ends.

Joseph and Christ

The Bible does not say that Joseph is a type of Christ, and, in my opinion, we are mistaken if we say that he is a type if the Bible is silent. Nevertheless, there are such remarkable parallels between Joseph and Christ that we cannot neglect to be taught by them.

The first parallel is that both were beloved of their father. The New Testament calls Jesus Christ the Son of the Father's love (Col. 1:13 ASV), a most profound and beautiful phrase. Joseph, too, had the special love of his father.

In contrast, both were hated by their brothers. Speaking of the Jews as God's special people, John wrote that

Jesus "came unto his own, and they that were his own received him not" (John 1:11, ASV). Similarly, when Joseph came over the hill to greet his brothers, they hated him.

The claims of both Christ and Joseph were rejected. Joseph's brothers did not believe his dreams; in fact, they hated him for mentioning them. Jesus spoke of his own rejection by the majority of the Jews in these terms:

> But all these things will they do unto you for my name's sake, because they know not him that sent me. If I had not come and spoken unto them, they had not had sin: but now they have no cloke for their sin. He that hateth me hateth my Father also. If I had not done among them the works which none other man did, they had not had sin: but now have they both seen and hated both me and my Father. (John 15:21-24)

They had seen Jesus in space and time, heard his propositional teaching and hated him. As Joseph's claims were rejected, so were Jesus'.

Each man had a price of silver placed upon him. And Joseph's brothers were quite *willing* to kill him, though they did not. The world reflected the same mentality when it fulfilled its willingness to kill Christ. I say the *world* killed Christ because not only the Jews were responsible, but Roman power and all mankind as well. Gentile and Jew alike, represented by the Jewish Sanhedrin and the Roman procurator, killed Jesus Christ. Rebellious mankind, you and I, killed Jesus Christ.

A Blessing to All People

Another interesting parallel between Joseph and Jesus is that thirty years of preparation preceded each man's central work. And each man's work resulted in a blessing to two classes of people. First, it was a blessing to their brethren. Joseph's family was saved from starvation because of what Joseph did. Jesus was a blessing to

his nation, the Jews. Speaking to Jews, with not a Gentile in sight, Peter said at Pentecost:
Repent and be baptized every one of you in the name of Jesus Christ for the remission of sins, and ye shall receive the gift of the Holy Spirit. For the promise is unto you, and to your children, and to all that are afar off, even as many as the Lord our God shall call. And with many other words did he testify and exhort, saying, Save yourselves from this untoward generation. Then they that gladly received his word were baptized: and the same day there were added unto them about three thousand souls. (Acts 2:38-41)
The early church was completely Jewish, the result of Jesus' ministry to his brethren. Some Jewish leaders were saved as well as many common people: "And the word of God increased; and the number of the disciples multiplied in Jerusalem greatly; and a great company of the priests were obedient to the faith" (Acts 6:7). There will be Jewish priests in heaven.

Second, the work of both Joseph and Jesus was a blessing to Gentiles. Joseph saved the whole nation of Egypt from starvation, and, happily, Christ's work did not end with the Jews either. God broke down the wall of partition between Gentile and Jew, as the gospel spread rapidly into the Graeco-Roman, the Gentile, world. Jews and Gentiles, Greeks and barbarians—all began to hear the good news preached to them.

Though it is a child's verse, this statement is profound: "Red and yellow, black and white, all are precious in his sight." Christ's salvation has spread to the Gentile as well as the Jew. He redeems to God people "out of every kindred, and tongue, and people, and nation" (Rev. 5:9). Before God's throne and before the Lamb will one day stand "a great multitude, which no man could number, of all nations, and kindreds, and peoples, and tongues" (Rev. 7:9).

We who are Gentiles should be thankful that the effect of Christ's work did not end with the Jews. Those of us who were not under the national covenant promises of God can stand before the throne if we cast ourselves on Christ. We should sing for joy! Some from every tribe and nation will be there upon the basis of what Christ has done. The primary lesson we learn from comparing Joseph and Christ is a lesson of salvation.

Joseph and David

Comparing Joseph and David teaches us a lesson about facing sin and temptation; it deals with our attitude toward temptation after we are Christians. Strong parallels exist between these two men's experience in that regard. Prior to the temptations we will compare, both had served God faithfully and had been placed in positions of power. Though David's power as king was greater than Joseph's in the house of Potiphar, both could do what they wanted to do without being challenged in the realm of their influence.

100

Joseph, you remember, was tempted by Potiphar's wife:

> His master's wife cast her eyes upon Joseph; and she said, Lie with me. But he refused, and said unto his master's wife, Behold, my master wotteth not what is with me in the house, and he hath committed all that he hath to my hand; There is none greater in this house than I; neither hath he kept back any thing from me but thee, because thou art his wife: how then can I do this great wickedness, and sin against God? And it came to pass, as she spake to Joseph day by day, that he hearkened not unto her, to lie by her, or to be with her. (Gen. 39:7-10)

Now read the history of David:

> And it came to pass, after the year was expired, at the time when kings go forth to battle, that David sent

Joab, and his servants with him, and all Israel; and they destroyed the children of Ammon, and besieged Rabbah. But David tarried still at Jerusalem. And it came to pass in an eveningtide, that David arose from off his bed, and walked upon the roof of the king's house: and from the roof he saw a woman washing herself; and the woman was very beautiful to look upon. And David sent and inquired after the woman. And one said, Is not this Bathsheba, the daughter of Eliam, the wife of Uriah the Hittite? And David sent messengers, and took her; and she came in unto him, and he lay with her; for she was purified from her uncleanness: and she returned unto her house. And the woman conceived, and sent and told David, and said, I am with child. (2 Sam. 11:1-5)

What was David's initial mistake? I would guess that he should have gone with the Lord's armies instead of sitting around in the affluence of power. As he was living in luxury while the Lord's armies were on the field of battle, he saw Bathsheba, lusted after her, wanted her and took her.

In contrast, Joseph said to the woman who tried to seduce him, "How then can I do this great wickedness, and sin against God?" (Gen. 39:9). Finally, "it came to pass about this time, that Joseph went into the house to do his business; and there was none of the men of the house there within. And she caught him by his garment, saying, Lie with me: and he left his garment in her hand, and fled, and got him out" (Gen. 39:11-12).

It would be difficult to conceive of a sharper antithesis than the way Joseph and David dealt with temptation. David toyed with sin; Joseph ran. Joseph would not even be with her (Gen. 39:10). So David sinned while Joseph escaped. Running is the only thing one can do when confronted by certain temptations.

David's sin was serious. Because God loved David, he

chastened him for it. And the bad effects of the sin continued for years. Not only did the child Bathsheba conceived die at birth, but the whole dilemma of Absalom and David's family situation was aggravated. It was a black mark on the history of the whole nation, a black mark on the ripples of history for years and years.

Thus, comparing Joseph and David teaches us what our attitude toward sin should be.

Joseph in Adversity

Joseph himself can teach us a lesson about how to deal with adversity. He experienced thirteen years of troubles. These troubles did not come upon him because of his own foolishness. Nor were they merely the turning of the wheels of a fallen world in history. First his brothers and then Potiphar's wife deliberately hurt him.

Joseph, however, saw God's hand in the midst of the trials. Though he never said that what his brothers had done was right, the mind-set through which he viewed his suffering made a tremendous difference in his life. After he had revealed himself to his brothers in Egypt, he said to them:

102

> Now therefore be not grieved, nor angry with yourselves, that ye sold me hither: for God did send me before you to preserve life. . . . And God sent me before you to preserve you a posterity in the earth, and to save your lives by a great deliverance. So now it was not you that sent me hither, but God: and he hath made me a father to Pharaoh, and lord of all his house, and a ruler throughout all the land of Egypt. (Gen. 45:5, 7-8)

When Jacob died, the brothers expected Joseph to take his vengeance, but even then Joseph said to them, "Fear not: for am I in the place of God? But as for you, ye thought evil against me; but God meant it unto good, to bring to pass, as it is this day, to save much people alive" (Gen. 50:19-20).

Even in adversity, Joseph truly lived in the presence of the God who is there. It was his practice, his attitude. Many of us would get tired after thirteen hours of adversity, but Joseph endured for thirteen *years!* Why? Because he understood that God really exists and that he is God even in the midst of wickedness and injustice.

Surely, most of us as Christians would want to have quietness, peace and usefulness like Joseph's in the midst of major adversity. And we can, because Scripture makes plain the conditions for this.

First, we must have Joseph's attitude toward temptation and sin. We must affirm that God exists and that hence his commands and our individual acts are meaningful. We need this perspective; we need to say in the face of temptation, "How can I do this great wickedness and sin against God?"

Second, we must, like Joseph, give God the glory at all times. Both in prison and before Pharaoh, Joseph's words rang out: "Do not interpretations belong to God? . . . It is not of me. . . . God has showed Pharaoh." While most men after years in prison would have quickly tried to enhance their own position, Joseph was careful to say first that God deserved the credit. Standing before his brothers and father he says, "God has made me lord of all Egypt." There must be a conscious choice as to who gets the glory when things are going well. This cannot be once for all; it must be moment by moment. This is a battle we never get beyond.

Third, we must be men of thankful hearts. Joseph gave God thanks for the comfort God provided in the midst of exile. When he called his first son Manasseh, he was giving thanks to God.

Because of his attitude toward sin and temptation, his conscious and careful choice to give God the glory and his being a man with a thankful heart, Joseph had peace

103

and usefulness in adversity. We, like Joseph, need to have a God-centered mind.

Imitating Joseph's Life

All of us, if we want to live a life like Joseph's in the midst of the confusion and blackness of our day, must learn the lessons taught by these three short sermons. The first, the lesson of Joseph and Christ, is a lesson of salvation. We cannot have any real peace of mind in this mixed-up world and mixed-up generation unless we cast ourselves upon Christ and personally accept his finished work. The second, the lesson of Joseph and David, teaches us to resist sin and temptation. The third, the lesson of Joseph in adversity, teaches us to be aware of God's *reality* at all times—both in the midst of the easy and the difficult.

We must learn these lessons as other lessons are learned. Spiritual muscles, like physical muscles, are made stronger through exercise. As we handle the smaller trials, we are prepared for the larger ones. If we cannot run with the footmen, we will never run with the horses.

If we learn the three lessons of Joseph, we will have peace and usefulness even in the midst of the last quarter of the twentieth century.

VII

The Ark, the Mercy Seat and the Incense Altar

Old Testament sacrifices could not make perfect in God's sight the worshipper who brought them, nor could they make his conscience completely free. The book of Hebrews makes this clear when it describes Old Testament worship as "a figure for the time then present, in which were offered both gifts and sacrifices, that could not make him that did the service perfect, as pertaining to the conscience; which stood only in meats and drinks, and divers washings, and carnal ordinances, imposed until the time of reformation" (Heb. 9:9-10).

But the writer of Hebrews goes on to say that *Christ* has become "an high priest of the good things to come, by a greater and more perfect tabernacle, not made with hands, that is to say, not of this creation" (Heb. 9:11). What the Old Testament sacrifices could not do, Christ had already done before the book of Hebrews was written. Old Testament worship in itself could not save.

It could not bring the conscience finally to rest. But Christ's sacrifice can.

Old Testament Sacrifice: An Illustration

Hebrews states that the Old Testament sacrifices were a *pattern* of what Christ later was to do in *fact*.

> It was therefore necessary that the patterns of the things in the heavens should be purified with these; but the heavenly things themselves with better sacrifices than these. For Christ entered not into a holy place made with hands, which are the figures of the true; but into heaven itself, now to appear in the presence of God for us. .... For the law having a shadow of the good things to come, and not the very image of the things, can never with those sacrifices which they offered continually make the comers thereunto perfect. (Heb. 9:23-24; 10:1)

The *the* before the words *good things* in the above quotations is important because in the Greek a definite article is used. The text is speaking not of a general idea but of a specific event for which the law provided a pattern, or illustration.

Interestingly enough, Old Testament worship as illustration is very much like the "happening" in contemporary art—not just a picture one looks at but a drama in which people are the actors. The Jews actually participated in this worship day after day, week after week, year after year. And, though the Old Testament worship could not in itself save, it nevertheless was a true worship as well as a profound illustration of eternal, spiritual truth.

The Heart of the Illustration

The heart of this illustration was the tabernacle and tabernacle worship. (The temple, as far as teaching is concerned, was only an extension of the tabernacle.)

According to Hebrews, "Moses was admonished of God when he was about to make the tabernacle: for, See, saith he, that thou make all things according to the pattern shewed to thee in the mount" (Heb. 8:5). The initial verb is actually stronger than *admonished*—it is *warned*. God said to Moses, "Don't you dare make it any other way. It's not your prerogative to change anything. Don't call in somebody who's going to make a different plan."

Stephen in Acts reiterates that the plan came from God: "Our fathers had the tabernacle of the witness in the wilderness, as he had appointed, speaking unto Moses, that he should make it according to the fashion that he had seen" (Acts 7:44). This place of worship was not built as a chapel or church building would be built today, for more than a human architect was involved. Moses was to follow a God-given pattern.

And Moses went into the midst of the cloud, and gat him up into the mount: and Moses was in the mount forty days and forty nights. (Ex. 24:18)

According to all that I shew thee, the pattern of the tabernacle, and the pattern of all the instruments thereof, even so shall ye make it. (Ex. 25:9)

And look that thou make them after their pattern, which thou wast caused to see in the mount. (Ex. 25:40)

And thou shalt rear up the tabernacle according to the fashion thereof that was shewed thee in the mount. (Ex. 26:30)

God gave Moses the plan for the tabernacle in a space-time, historic situation on Mount Sinai. God himself was the architect, causing Moses to see a vision (or something of this nature) and saying, "Here is what the tabernacle is to be like, exactly like this and not otherwise!"

We cannot stress too much that *God* gave the pattern and that he gave it in order to provide a correct picture

109

of Christ and his work. For, if it was to be a pattern of what was to come, it could not be left to men's minds to think it up. God had to give it so that it would be an adequate illustration (in the living, deep sense of illustration mentioned above) of what Christ would do. The points we have seen so far are (1) Old Testament worship was not sufficient in itself, and (2) it was a God-given, correct pattern of what Christ would do.

The Ark

If a person were to walk into and through the tabernacle, he would come first into a court made by curtains, then into a tent and, finally, at the end of the tent, into a separate compartment called the Holy of Holies. In Exodus 25:10, God begins to reveal the things which were to be placed within the structure, starting with the ark in the Holy of Holies: "And they shall make an ark of acacia wood: two cubits and a half shall be the length thereof, and a cubit and a half the breadth thereof, and a cubit and a half the height thereof."

It is interesting that God described everything (with one exception of which we shall speak later) from the Holy of Holies outward. This means that the tabernacle was not to be viewed from the perspective of the worshipper but from the perspective of God, as he would see it from his declared special presence in the Holy of Holies. The order was from the Holy of Holies flowing outward.

The ark itself represented the presence of God, and to the Jews it was their most precious possession. We should note that no idol was placed with the ark or put anywhere else inside or outside the tabernacle. According to tradition, when Pompey entered the temple and forced his way into the Holy of Holies, he snorted, "They don't even have a god," because he found no idol there. A Greek or Roman or Etruscan temple had in general the same sort of construction as the tabernacle in that it had an inner, smaller sacred place, but its sacred place always contained an idol. In Exodus, therefore, we see something profound: No idol was placed in the Holy of Holies.

Rather, God placed the ark there as a representation of his *character*. The important thing is what the content of God's character is. And that content is represented in the ark.

This representation of God's character had two parts, the first being the ark itself. Basically, the ark was just a box, though, because it was made of acacia wood and overlaid with gold, a heavy and precious box. It was made as a box in order to contain something, namely, the law of God: "And thou shalt put into the ark the testimony which I shall give thee" (Ex. 25:16). This "testimony" was the Ten Commandments; and then there existed the other portions of God's law which were extensions of the Ten Commandments.

Central, therefore, was a statement of the law of God —the law which declared his holiness. The law reflects what God's character *is*. It is not just what he commands men to do in order to establish some kind of sociological form. The comprehension of who God is begins with an understanding of his character. God is a holy God, God continues to be a holy God, God will always be a holy God.

The Mercy Seat

If the box and the law it contained were the only representation of God's character, the Jews would still have been left with their sin. Confronted solely with God's perfection, they would have remained without hope. But immediately the box was completed: "And thou shalt make a mercy seat of pure gold: two cubits and a half shall be the length thereof, and a cubit and a half the breadth thereof" (Ex. 25:17). This "mercy seat" was the lid, the second part of the ark. A very important thing, this lid.

It was Luther, when translating the Old Testament into German, who first used the term *mercy seat*. It is a beautiful, poetic phrase—but it also accurately communicates what the lid on the ark really was, a place of mercy. Yet if a person does not know the Hebrew word being translated, *mercy seat* may confuse, because this word actually means *the propitiation, the propitiatory, the covering*—a covering not like a jar lid, but a covering in the sense of atonement. This is emphasized by the fact that Hebrews 9:5, in speaking of the "cherubims of glory shadowing the mercy seat," uses a Greek word which means *the propitiatory*. Our hearts should well up when we consider Luther's poetic translation of the term, and yet we must understand the term's real force, **112** *the propitiatory, the atonement*.

The propitiatory covering was exactly the same size as the box. They matched. The atonement exactly covered the law. Here, I feel, is the balance we find in the New Testament—the balance of the character of God. God is holy (he is always holy, he never ceases being holy) and God is love. Both must be affirmed.

God is holy, God is love. Neither is primary, neither is secondary. If a person understands the character of God, he knows *both* "God is holy" *and* "God is love." We can reverse the statements, and it is well to do so in our conversation and thought in order to remind ourselves that one is not above the other. The character of God is this: He is holy, he is love, he is love, he is holy. These two stand together as the character of God.

Notice that the command to put the law into the box is immediately prior to the command to make the mercy seat (Ex. 25:16-17). That this linkage is not merely a flowing of the literary form is indicated by the fact that these two are again connected in verse 21: "And thou shalt put the mercy seat above upon the ark; and in the ark thou shalt put the testimony that I shall give thee." And this ties in expressly with the following verse: "And there I will meet with thee, and I will commune with thee from above the mercy seat, from between the two cherubims which are upon the ark of the testimony, of all things which I will give thee in commandment unto the children of Israel" (Ex. 25:22). Two times the law in the box is mentioned in the context of the covering (the propitiatory, the atonement) that is to be upon it.

Meeting God at the Mercy Seat
Verse 22 contains an important clause: "and there I will meet with thee." God did not meet the Jews at the level of the law. He met them at the level of the mercy seat. Undoubtedly, this is why Luther, loving the Lord as he did, called the covering the *mercy seat.* He understood that this is where God meets everybody who is met by him.

113

If we had the law only, we would share the fate of Uzza, whom God killed because he touched the ark, even though Uzza had the intent of keeping it from falling over when the oxen pulling it stumbled (1 Chron. 13:9-10). To come to God on the basis of the law would mean to be separated from God for eternity. But God does not confront us only with the box and the law therein. He brings us to the mercy seat, and there, at the place of atonement, meets with us graciously and gently.

The book of Exodus teaches this lesson in other ways. For instance, in Exodus 20:24, when the first mention is made of an altar after the giving of the law, we read:

An altar of earth thou shalt make unto me, and shalt sacrifice thereon thy burnt offerings, and thy peace offerings, thy sheep, and thine oxen: in all places where I record my name I will come unto thee, and I will bless thee. And if thou wilt make me an altar of stone, thou shalt not build it of hewn stone: for if thou lift up thy tool upon it, thou has polluted it. (Ex. 20:24-25)

When he gave this first altar to the Jewish people after giving them the law, God clearly said that they would not be able to come to him on the basis of any beauty they themselves would give it. The altar was to be of either earth or rough stone without a tool mark on it. (Later the brazen altar was given for the tabernacle but that was in a different situation.) The emphasis here is that if any human tool touches this altar, the altar will be spoiled.

Exodus 24:4-8 also illustrates that the Jews came to God on the basis of his mercy and not on the basis of the law:

> And Moses wrote all the words of the LORD, and rose up early in the morning, and builded an altar under the mount, and twelve pillars, according to the twelve tribes of Israel. And he sent young men of the children of Israel, which offered burnt offerings, and sacrificed peace offerings of oxen unto the LORD. And Moses took half of the blood, and put it in basons; and half of the blood he sprinkled on the altar. And he took the book of the covenant, and read in the audience of the people: and they said, All that the LORD hath said will we do, and be obedient. And Moses took the blood, and sprinkled it on the people, and said, Behold the blood of the covenant, which the LORD hath made with you concerning all these words.

In this section, the book of the covenant and the blood of the covenant stand together. In order to have knowledge, man needs the revelation of this book, that is, he needs contentful, propositional communication; and in order to have forgiveness, man needs the shedding of this blood. No covenant is possible between God—holy, perfect, morally absolute forever—and a revolted man-

114

kind except on the basis of the blood of the covenant.

The day of atonement portrayed in the book of Leviticus also relates to our discussion. On this one day each year, the High Priest entered the Holy of Holies and sprinkled blood *on the mercy seat*, as God had commanded (Lev. 16:14). Surely, God was again connecting the idea of the propitiatory, the atonement, with the shedding of blood. There is a relationship between this day of the sprinkling of blood and that great picture of the coming of Jesus, the mercy seat.

Leviticus also states that the fire carried into God's presence on the day of atonement was to come from a specific situation. The High Priest "shall take a censer full of burning coals of fire from off the altar before the LORD" (Lev. 16:12). The fire was to come from the altar and nowhere else. Anything else was "strange fire." Two sons of Aaron, Nadab and Abihu, tried to offer such "strange fire," and God immediately struck them **115** down with fire (Lev. 10:1-2).

We see, then, that the truth that God is met on his terms at the level of the mercy seat is found not only in a small portion of Exodus. It is not an isolated concept. It is the very warp and woof of everything that touches upon this subject. God told the Jews, "There I will meet with thee, and I will commune with thee from above the mercy seat" (Ex. 25:22). God meets his people from the mercy seat, not from the law.

I think that the apostle Paul had this expressly in mind when he wrote the wonderful third chapter of Romans. There he described Christ as the one "whom God hath set forth to be a propitiation through faith in his blood, to declare his righteousness for the remission of sins that are past" (Rom. 3:25). The Greek actually says something stronger than "a propitiation." It says that God sent forth Christ to be *the propitiatory*, exactly what the lid on the ark had been called.

Christ is the propitiatory. And Paul, being a Jew well versed in Jewish thought, was, I feel, referring back to the top of the ark, back to the mercy seat, and saying to the Jews in Rome, as well as to the Gentiles who needed to learn deeper truth, that Christ is in *reality* what the propitiatory in the Old Testament was (to use the words of Hebrews) as a *figure*, a *pattern*, a *picture* of the things to come.

On this basis, and no other, Romans 3:26 has meaning: "To declare, I say, at this time his righteousness: that he might be just, and the justifier of him which believeth in Jesus." We cannot meet God at the level of the law, his holiness of character. But we can meet him on the basis of that which the covering of the ark represents —Christ doing a propitiatory work. God, therefore, can remain holy and yet justify those who have faith in Jesus. And thus in the tabernacle there is a box with the law covered by the propitiatory.

The Brazen Altar

After describing the ark, God commands the making of a table of acacia wood (Ex. 25:23). This is a table for the shewbread, which through the years has been interpreted as representing Christ as the Bread of Life, whom a person feeds upon after becoming a Christian. The next item God describes is a lampstand (Ex. 25:31), which has often, and I think correctly, been thought to relate to Christ, the Light of the World. Interestingly, this lampstand was the only light in the tabernacle; without it, the tabernacle would have been dark. So Jesus too is the only light of the world.

As we come to chapter 27, we have passed from the Holy of Holies through the tent itself (which chapter 26 has described) into the courtyard. The first thing a person would see as he approached the tent from the outside would be the brazen altar on which the sacrifices were made: "And thou shalt make an altar of acacia wood, five cubits long, and five cubits broad; the altar shall be foursquare: and the height thereof shall be three cubits. And thou shalt make the horns of it upon the four corners thereof: his horns shall be of the same: and thou shalt overlay it with brass" (Ex. 27:1-2).

This altar stood outside the tent at the only way of entrance, for the sacrifice, as we have seen, was the only approach to God and was tied in specifically with the blood sprinkled upon the mercy seat. On that marvelous and unique day of atonement, once a year, a basin of blood was carried with great care from the altar and taken, along with a censer full of fire from the altar, into the Holy of Holies. The High Priest passed through the Holy Place, pushed aside the curtain and entered the Holy of Holies. Only the priest actually entered, but by representation the people also entered. Having come into the presence of God with the blood and with fire **117** from the altar, he sprinkled the blood on the mercy seat.

In addition to the sacrifice on the day of atonement, the Jews were to sacrifice two lambs on the altar every day, one lamb in the morning and one in the evening (Ex. 29:38-39). And there were to be many other sacrifices on the altar. There was to be a continued application of the blood.

It is important to understand that this was not just a dry worship on a formal level. The sacrifices were to lead to an end: "And I will dwell among the children of Israel, and will be their God. And they shall know that I am the LORD their God, that brought them forth out of the land of Egypt, that I may dwell among them: I am the LORD their God" (Ex. 29:45-46). The purpose of these sacrifices was not formalistic worship, not even as a picture of the coming of Christ. They were performed so that God would now dwell among his people, meeting them at the mercy seat.

The Incense Altar

At the beginning of chapter 30, the movement from the Holy of Holies outward is interrupted. Two items in the tent were described back in chapter 25—the lampstand and the table of shewbread. In Exodus 30:1, God describes another piece of furniture in the tent, in the Holy Place, namely, the incense altar.

Why is the incense altar out of place in the description? The reason, I think, is this. The incense altar was the place of prayer and praise, and therefore it is described out of order to communicate this great lesson: Acceptable praise and worship are the last things. They come at the end of all the rest.

We read in Psalm 141 these wonderful words: "Let my prayer be set forth before thee as incense; and the lifting up of my hands as the evening sacrifice" (Ps. 141:2). David understood that prayer and incense, the rising of the incense from the incense altar, are related. The book of Revelation also speaks of the prayers of the saints as incense rising.

Where in the tabernacle was this altar of praise and worship placed? "And thou shalt put it before the vail that is by the ark of the testimony, before the mercy seat that is over the testimony, where I will meet with thee" (Ex. 30:6). Though the incense altar was set outside the Holy of Holies in front of the veil, clearly the point was that the prayer and worship were to be offered up before the mercy seat. The incense altar was put outside the veil only for practical reasons—the High Priest could only go into the Holy of Holies once a year but incense was to be burned daily.

The incense altar also had a relationship to the shedding of blood, for God commanded that "Aaron shall make an atonement upon the horns of it [the incense altar] once in a year with the blood of the sin offering ot atonements" (Ex. 30:10). A man's natural worship violates God's character. To worship acceptably we must come on the basis of propitiation. Even the incense altar, even the praise and the worship, had to be cleansed with the shedding of blood.

Just as "strange fire" was forbidden, so "strange incense" could not be offered (Ex. 30:9). A person was forbidden to bring "strange" praise to God. He had to come in the way God had prescribed, conforming to who God is and the way God has opened. We today cannot bring acceptable worship and prayer to God unless we see him as he has revealed himself in the Scripture and as he has provided forgiveness in the historic solution of Christ's death upon the cross.

I do not mean that God never hears an unsaved man who cries out, "Be merciful to me a sinner." But people of the world are absolutely wrong in thinking they can praise God in their own way. This strange incense is unacceptable. Let us not get the order reversed. It is not a favor to God to give him praise and worship, whether in a formal worship service or through the praise of a life. If a man says he is going to praise God with his formal attendance at a service or with his life and thinks he is doing God a favor or purchasing some divine good will, he is absolutely mistaken.

God has ordained an order for worship, not one which is arbitrary but one which conforms to who he is. In Old Testament times, the representation of his character was in the Holy of Holies. So what was needed first was that which met his holiness. Consequently, the first thing every man had to do to approach God was to pass by the brazen altar. Hebrews says that the Holy Spirit was "signifying that the way into the holiest of all was not yet made manifest, while as the first tabernacle was yet standing" (Heb. 9:8). This means that the Holy Spirit made plain (from the continual offering needed in Old Testament times, for the priests and then for the people)

119

that the way into the Holy of Holies was not yet truly open. This is connected with the fact that when Jesus died the veil of the temple was torn from top to bottom. In tearing the veil, God was saying, "The pattern is needed no longer. The reality has come. Christ has died, the offering is given; it is quite finished. Christ the Savior has come." In Christ's sacrifice, the true propitiatory has come to pass. The holiness of God is not made null; God is still the holy God—but the propitiatory work of Christ has covered our guilt once for all.

Thus, those who wish to come to God must pass by the brazen altar first. We today must follow not merely the pattern but the reality; we must accept Christ and his propitiatory work.

Applying Christ's Finished Work

Unlike the Old Testament sacrifices, which had to be offered continually, Christ died only once. The Greek is very strong: He died once for all. His death was final and sufficient.

And almost all things are by the law purged with blood, and without shedding of blood is no remission. It was therefore necessary that the patterns of things in the heavens should be purified with these; but the heavenly things themselves with better sacrifices than these. For Christ is not entered into the holy places made with hands, which are the figures of the true; but into heaven itself, now to appear in the presence of God for us: Nor yet that he should offer himself often, as the high priest entereth into the holy place every year with blood of others; For then must he often have suffered since the foundation of the world: but now once for all in the end of the world hath he appeared to put away sin by the sacrifice of himself. And as it is appointed unto men once to die, but after this the judgment: So Christ was once for all offered to bear the sins of many; and unto them that look for him shall he appear the second time without sin unto salvation. (Heb. 9:22-28)

But let us be careful. Because Christ died only once and because I accept him as my Savior only once does not mean that his blood is to be applied only once. The Old Testament morning and evening sacrifices still have something to say to us. The shewbread for example, tells us that Christ is not to be fed on only once, but daily, existentially. Christ, the Light of the World, is to be my light not only on the day of my justification and conversion; he is to be my light existentially, every moment of my life.

The two great sacraments emphasize this. The Old Testament circumcision and New Testament baptism represent a once-for-all thing. But the other sacrament, the Passover in the Old Testament and the Lord's Supper in the New, is something that is repeated throughout one's life. The first is representative of the once-for-allness of the work of Christ when I accept him as my Savior, the second the constant relationship with the One who is there. Feeding upon Christ in our hearts by faith does not negate the once-for-allness of salvation. There is a difference between being saved once-for-all and applying daily, through faith, the finished work of Christ. I must look to the finished work of Christ in the *now* of my life.

The shed blood of the Lamb of God is not "useful" to me only for justification. As it is applied moment by moment, I am able to be at the mercy seat continuously. Even though I have been converted once-for-all, if I am not now consciously laying hold of the finished work of Christ, the blood of the Lamb of God, for my sacrifice, I cannot expect the experience of meeting God at the mercy seat to be real. Meeting God at the mercy seat rests upon the once-for-all finished work of Christ on the cross, but the application of that finished work is to be a constant thing in my life. If I am constantly applying that blood, then there can be a real and experiential meeting with God at the mercy seat now.

And now finally I am ready for the incense altar. Remember the order in Exodus. The incense altar was given after God had said, "Now I will dwell among you." The same order must be true with me. I am not ready for either public or private worship if I have not asked God's cleansing from any sin presently in my life. My life cannot be a praise to God until this cleansing is a reality.

If my worship is to be real, and not just outward form, then two things must take place first. There must be the once-for-all propitiatory cleansing of the blood of Christ for my justification. And there must be the *now* cleansing which is brought about by laying hold in faith of the finished work of Christ. Then I have opened to me an open relationship with God at the mercy seat.

Then I am ready to praise God, both in a formal worship service and in my life.

VIII

David:
Lawful
and
Unlawful
Vindication

David is a very special man in Scripture. When God chose him as a young man to replace the unfaithful Saul as king, God described him as "a man after his own heart" (1 Sam. 13:14). David was a man who prayed much and often. He created some of the world's most beautiful poems, many of which were used as songs in the liturgical services of the temple. The book of Acts (2:25, 30) identifies him as a prophet, too. At times he spoke not just in his own wisdom, but inspired by the Holy Spirit he revealed facts about the coming Messiah.

David's Sin
But David was not perfect. The Bible is a realistic book—not that it portrays only the dirt in life (like "realism" today) but that it portrays men as they actually are. It shows imperfections in each biblical character whose life it records with any fullness.

When we think of David's weakness, we immediately recall his sin with Bathsheba:

And it came to pass, after the year was expired, at the time when kings go forth to battle, that David sent Joab, and his servants with him, and all Israel; and they destroyed the children of Ammon, and besieged Rabbah. But David tarried still at Jerusalem. And it came to pass in an eveningtide, that David arose from off his bed, and walked upon the roof of the king's house: and from the roof he saw a woman washing herself; and the woman was very beautiful to look upon. And David sent and enquired after the woman. And one said, Is not this Bathsheba, the daughter of Eliam, the wife of Uriah the Hittite? And David sent messengers, and took her; and she came in unto him, and he lay with her; for she was purified from her uncleanness: and she returned unto her house. And the woman conceived, and sent and told David, and said, I am with child. (2 Sam. 11:1-5)

The armies of Israel were in the field, but King David, rather than being with the army, was sitting in his palace. He did not sin in seeing Bathsheba because he did not seek to do so, but he was wrong to initiate the steps which led to his sexual relationship with her.

When David learned Bathsheba was pregnant, he acted to cover up his sin. His plan was very simple. Uriah was named as one of the valiant men in David's army (1 Chron. 11:41). David ordered Uriah sent to him from the field of battle and then told Uriah to return to his own house. He expected Uriah to spend a number of days with Bathsheba and therefore think the child was his own. But David ran into an unexpected difficulty: "Uriah slept at the door of the king's house with all the servants of his lord, and went not down to his house" (2 Sam. 11:9). Uriah wanted to identify with the forces of Israel at war rather than to dwell at ease.

126

Surely this was God speaking to David if David would have listened, but instead he pursued his plan. David made Uriah drunk, thinking he then would go to his wife: "And when David had called him, he did eat and drink before him; and he made him drunk: and at even he went out to lie on his bed with the servants of his lord, but went not down to his house" (2 Sam. 11:13). So David took the next step in his sin: "David wrote a letter to Joab, and sent it by the hand of Uriah. And he wrote in the letter, saying, Set ye Uriah in the forefront of the hottest battle, and retire ye from him, that he may be smitten, and die" (2 Sam. 11:14-15). It was an especially horrible thing to send such a message by Uriah's own hand. A clever plan—Go ahead, Joab, have him killed—which was exactly what happened. Joab soon sent a word to David which taunted him and highlighted David's deceitfulness. Joab instructed his messenger, saying, "Tell David that some people were killed near the wall of the city we were attacking. When he says, 'Joab, you're a fool. Why did you get so close to the wall?' then spring the trap on him. Say, 'Your servant Uriah the Hittite is dead, too' " (2 Sam. 11:21).

When Bathsheba heard the news, she mourned for her husband, but "when the mourning was past, David sent and fetched her to his house, and she became his wife, and bare him a son" (2 Sam. 11:27). Everything was now in good order in the society. The baby would be born and have a father. Everything was normal except for one thing: What David had done was evil in the eyes of the Lord. God said "It's sin" and sent his prophet Nathan to David:

And he came unto him, and said unto him, There were two men in one city; the one rich, and the other poor. The rich man had exceeding many flocks and herds: But the poor man had nothing, save one little ewe lamb, which he had bought and nourished up:

and it grew up together with him, and with his children; it did eat of his own food, and drank of his own cup, and lay in his bosom, and was unto him as a daughter. And there came a traveller unto the rich man, and he spared to take of his own flock and of his own herd, to dress for the wayfaring man that was come unto him; but took the poor man's lamb, and dressed it for the man that was come to him. And David's anger was greatly kindled against the man; and he said to Nathan, As the LORD liveth, the man that hath done this thing shall surely die: And he shall restore the lamb fourfold, because he did this thing, and because he had no pity. (2 Sam. 12:1-6)

This was David—king of the people of God and therefore judge and mediator of the law of Moses—thinking properly. The law of God, which was not only the Jews' religious law but also their civil law, was in operation, and David had spoken as judge. His words were incisive—"because he had no pity." But Nathan turned the matter and put David on trial: "Thou art the man" (2 Sam. 12:7). Nathan did not charge David primarily with adultery, though adulterer he had been. He charged David with murder: "Wherefore hast thou despised the commandment of the LORD, to do evil in his sight? thou hast killed Uriah the Hittite with the sword, and hast taken his wife to be thy wife, and hast slain him with the sword of the children of Ammon" (2 Sam. 12:9).

David was not brought face to face with some humanitarian principle. He was confronted with the eternal law of God: "thou [hast] despised the commandment of the Lord." That he was one step removed from the killing did not change God's judgment. David had committed murder just as though he had taken his own sword and run Uriah through. Nathan reminded David that he had violated God's law (his sin was not just against society), and then he prophesied, "Now therefore the sword shall never depart from thine house; because thou hast despised me" (2 Sam. 12:10). In despising the commandment of the Lord, David had despised the Lord himself. There is no difference: To despise one is to despise the other. David had despised the law of God which as king it was his calling to administer.

David was sorry and responded by making his great confession: "I have sinned against the LORD" (2 Sam. 12:13). He wrote the fifty-first psalm, a psalm of confession.

Have mercy upon me, O God, according to thy lovingkindness: according unto the multitude of thy tender mercies blot out my transgressions. Wash me thoroughly from mine iniquity, and cleanse me from my sin. For I acknowledge my transgressions: and my sin is ever before me. Against thee, thee only, have I sinned, and done this evil in thy sight: that thou mightest be justified when thou speakest, and be clear when thou judgest. Behold, I was shapen in iniquity; and in sin did my mother conceive me. Behold, thou desirest truth in the inward parts: and in the hidden part thou shalt make me to know wisdom. Purge me with hyssop, and I shall be clean: wash me, and I shall be whiter than snow. (Ps. 51:1-7)

After David's confession, God said to him through Nathan, "The LORD also hath put away thy sin; thou shalt not die" (2 Sam. 12:13). God was not going to strike David down for his sin, but neither was he going to prevent it from affecting the flow of history: "Howbeit, because by this deed thou hast given great occasion to the enemies of the LORD to blaspheme, the child also that is born unto thee shall surely die" (2 Sam. 12:13). The Judeo-Christian world view emphasizes the reality of history and the significance of men in history. History progresses; the things we do have their effect in history.

So ripples continued from David's sin. The child begotten by David and Bathsheba died. But that is not the only result. There are results in David's own family. The Bible itself makes clear this cause-and-effect relationship, for in 2 Samuel 12:11-12 we read, "Behold, I will raise up evil against thee out of thine own house, and I will take thy wives before thine eyes and give them unto thy neighbour and he shall lie with the wives in the sight of this sun. For thou didst it secretly but I will do this thing before all Israel, and before the sun." This was fulfilled literally when Absalom went into David's concubines (2 Sam. 16:21). David sinned in secret with Bathsheba; Absalom's monstrous sin was open before all men. The ripples of David's sin flowed on and on.

Amnon, one of David's oldest sons, committed sexual sin with his half-sister Tamar, and then, as if this were not bad enough, shoved her out of the house and slammed the door in her face—an act so heartless and cruel it could only spring from a fallen race. Botticelli's *Abandoned*, painted in his later period after he had been influenced by Savonarola, portrays a woman weeping outside a shut door, and I have no doubt that he was picturing Tamar. But why shouldn't Amnon commit a cruel sexual sin like this? After all, hadn't his father? A destructive principle had been fixed in David's family. Later Absalom murdered Amnon. Why not? Had not David taught his family to use murder as a weapon?

Non-Vindication in Personal Matters

Two things come together here. The first is David's principle of *non-vindication in personal matters*.

David operated in this way with Saul. Once while Saul was chasing him, seeking to destroy him, David had an excellent opportunity to kill Saul, and David's own men urged him on, "Behold the day of which the LORD said unto thee, Behold, I will deliver thine enemy into thine hand, that thou mayest do to him as it shall seem good unto thee" (1 Sam. 24:4). "Quick," the men said. "He's vulnerable. Saul is asleep, all his guards are asleep, just thrust once with your spear, David, and it's all over." But David simply cut off a part of Saul's robe and left him. Later he called out to Saul across a valley, "The LORD judge between me and thee, and the LORD avenge me of thee: but mine hand shall not be upon thee" (1 Sam. 24:12). A striking statement of non-vindication in a personal matter! The Bible specifically brings this out as a principle in David's relationship to Nabal and Abigail. David, still being pursued by Saul, had become expert at guerrilla warfare. Naturally, he and his men had to eat, and rather than earn their living by robbery (because David loved the LORD) they provided protection for shepherds against thieves. In return, they expected to be fed—a reasonable arrangement.

In doing this, David and his men ran into Nabal. **131** Though Nabal's own shepherds testified that David and his men, hungry or not, had not stolen one sheep, Nabal foolishly told David, "You get nothing." David set out to administer punishment on Nabal but happily was stopped by Abigail, Nabal's wife, who said to him, "Nabal is a fool but count his error against me." I think the conversation which followed indicates clearly that everyone knew that David on principle did not vindicate himself. This was his reputation that had spread over the mountainsides. Abigail faced him with it: "That this shall be no grief unto thee, nor offence of heart unto my lord, either that thou hast shed blood causeless, or that my lord hath avenged himself: but when the LORD shall have dealt well with my lord, then remember thine handmaid" (1 Sam. 25:31). In other words, she said, "I'm here to keep you straight on your principle. In your anger, you're close to deserting it. I've come to remind you not to make the mistake of avenging yourself because later you'll be overwhelmingly sorry."

David was grateful for the reminder: "Blessed be the LORD God of Israel, which sent thee this day to meet me: And blessed be thy advice, and blessed be thou, which hast kept me this day from coming to shed blood, and from avenging myself with mine own hand" (1 Sam. 25:32-33). "Thanks be to God," said David. "I hear the voice of God in your words, and I will stop short. I will let God do the avenging."

At this particular place we should think of Psalm 37 because it states David's principle:

Fret not thyself because of evildoers, neither be thou envious against the workers of iniquity. For they shall soon be cut down like the grass, and wither as the green herb. Trust in the LORD, and do good; so shalt thou dwell in the land, and verily thou shalt be fed. Delight thyself also in the LORD; and he shall give thee the desires of thine heart.... Rest in the LORD, and wait patiently for him: fret not thyself because of him who prospereth in his way, because of the man who bringeth wicked devices to pass. Cease from anger, and forsake wrath: fret not thyself in any wise to do evil. For evildoers shall be cut off: but those that wait upon the LORD, they shall inherit the earth. For yet a little while, and the wicked shall not be: yea, thou shalt diligently consider his place, and it shall not be. But the meek shall inherit the earth; and shall delight themselves in the abundance of peace. (Ps. 37:1-4, 7-11)

In the Beatitudes, Jesus quotes the words "the meek shall inherit the earth" to point out the beautiful virtue of not vindicating oneself (Mt. 5:5). David practiced this virtue—not perfectly, I am sure, but as a general principle. It was not that David did not care about the justice of the situation, but he believed the Lord would bring it to pass.

In the incident with Nabal, David's waiting upon the Lord was fulfilled. God judged the wicked man, and his judgment this time was more immediate than is often the case: "And it came to pass about ten days after, that the LORD smote Nabal, that he died. And when David heard that Nabal was dead, he said, Blessed be the LORD, that hath pleaded the cause of my reproach from the hand of Nabal, and hath kept his servant from evil" (1 Sam. 25:38-39).

On another occasion, Saul again was in David's hands. God, in his providence, twice put Saul where David could kill him. David said, "Destroy him not: for who can stretch forth his hand against the LORD's anointed, and be guiltless? . . . As the LORD liveth, the LORD shall smite him; or his day shall come to die; or he shall descend into battle, and perish. The LORD forbid that I should stretch forth mine hand against the LORD's anointed" (1 Sam. 26:9-11).

Even after Saul's death, David was careful to put into practice the principle of non-vindication. Instead of saying "Hurrah! Hurrah!" David acknowledged his own place before God and did something overwhelmingly beautiful:

And the king said, Is there not yet any of the house of Saul, that I may shew the kindness of God unto him? And Ziba said unto the king, Jonathan hath yet a son, which is lame on his feet. . . . Then king David sent, and fetched him out of the house of Machir, the son of Ammiel, from Lodebar. . . . And David said unto him, Fear not: for I will surely shew thee kindness for Jonathan thy father's sake, and will restore thee all the land of Saul thy father; and thou shalt eat bread at my table continually. (2 Sam. 9:3, 5, 7)

The principle of non-vindication in personal matters is, I think, more accurately illustrated in these acts of David than in those of anyone else in Scripture except our Lord Jesus himself. David showed something beautiful, something good—the turning of the other cheek in a personal matter. I suspect that especially after his sin with Bathsheba he would have been more sympathetic, in a good sense, to human weakness. He would have become more inclined to say "*we* are sinners" rather than "*you* are a sinner"—and that is good.

The Flaw in David's Response

There was a flaw in David's response to Amnon, however, which distorted what in itself was good. When David heard that Amnon had had intercourse with his half-sister Tamar and had cruelly shoved her out of the door, "he was very wroth" (2 Sam. 13:21). That's fair enough; of course he should be angry. But, because people knew about his sin with Bathsheba, he was in a poor position, both as king and father, to do anything about it. And he did not jump over this difficulty (which existed because of his own sin) and punish the offense: He became angry but did nothing. If David had punished this sin rightly, perhaps Absalom, another of David's sons, would not have taken it upon himself to punish it wrongly. For Absalom murdered his half-brother Amnon—not with his own hand but through the hand of his servant.

Then Absalom fled, leaving David's jurisdiction so David could do nothing about his offense, and Joab used subterfuge to have Absalom brought back into Jerusalem. Joab was a pragmatist. No principles, please; let's get this thing running and running well. He had a woman from Tekoa come to David with a trumped up story. "One of my sons has killed another," she said, "and the rest of the family is insisting he be killed." According to the law of God, this family may have been heartless, lacking tears and acting proudly, without love or sorrow for the woman, but they were right in what they demanded. If we miss this, we miss everything. The law of God says that murder is to be punished.

David, however, responded by saying, "As the LORD liveth, there shall not one hair of thy son fall to the earth" (2 Sam. 14:11), and his wrong judgment in relation to this fabricated story trapped him when he later faced the real situation of Absalom's murder of Amnon. He was not a private individual who could just say to the woman, "Poor thing, I'm so sorry for you." He was the supreme judge of Israel, the supreme court of the land, the upholder of the law of God, and murder should have been punished. As judge he was wrong in saying, "Just skip it." He was really saying, "Forget the law."

In response to the woman's fabricated story, he set aside the law of God, so when the situation with Absalom was brought forward, he was caught. He had no recourse unless he chose to reverse himself, but, just as in his previous failure to punish Amnon, he did not jump over what was against him in order to do what was right. His principle of non-vindication plus his gentleness and understanding of human weakness was good, but it became wrong when he said, "Forget the law of God." We cannot state it any less bluntly.

After David had made his judgment, in regard to the fabricated story, the woman said to him, "For we must needs die, and are as water spilt on the ground, which cannot be gathered up again" (2 Sam. 14:14), and immediately David knew Joab, the pragmatist, had tricked him. How did he know? Because these words echoed the words he had spoken to Joab about the death of Uriah (2 Sam. 11:25). David was caught, but the situation was still not impossible. He could have remembered the law of God and his calling as king of Israel and judge of the people of God, and he could have cried out, "God, have mercy on me! I have been wrong but now I stand." He did not.

135

Even before the woman saw him, though, something was wrong, for "the soul of King David longed to go forth unto Absalom: for he was comforted concerning Amnon, seeing he was dead" (2 Sam. 13:39). This was exactly what Joab had the woman say, "After all, after a man is dead, what then?" Well, the law of God still remains.

This is very different from what occurred after Bathsheba's child died. Immediately after the birth, David fasted and cried out to God, "Can't my child live?" But when David, being a wise man, saw the servants talking among themselves, he knew exactly what it meant: The child was dead and they were afraid to tell him. Therefore, David said to them,

Is the child dead? And they said, He is dead. Then David arose from the earth, and washed, and anointed himself, and changed his apparel, and came into the house of the LORD, and worshipped: then he came to his own house; and when he required, they set bread before him, and he did eat. Then said his servants unto him, What thing is this that thou hast done? thou didst fast and weep for the child, while it was alive; but when the child was dead, thou didst rise and eat bread. And he said, While the child was yet alive, I fasted and wept: for I said, Who can tell whether GOD will be gracious to me, that the child may live? But now he is dead, wherefore should I fast? can I bring him back again? I shall go to him, but he shall not return to me. (2 Sam. 12:19-23)

This was a tremendous virtue. David knew God to be merciful, so as long as the child was alive he kept praying and fasting. As soon as the child was dead, though, he responded, "Someday I'll die and see him again. I'll go to him, then, but he won't come to me now from the dead, for death is death. The matter is finished. Give me something to eat." This is beautiful beyond words.

When David expressed these same sentiments regarding Absalom, however, the situation was not the same, and David was no longer virtuous. The baby had died a natural death—as chastisement to David, yes, but a natural death nonetheless. Amnon had not died this way; Absalom had murdered him. When a man dies of natural causes, the door is shut, the thing is finished. But when one man stands as the murderer of another, the law of God remains. We are not faced with sociological considerations alone. We are faced with an eternal God who has given us a law that shows his own character. David forgot this law. So what had been a virtue now became open sin! Therefore, it is not surprising that David said to Joab, "Behold now, I have done this thing: go therefore, bring the young man Absalom again" (2 Sam. 14:21). The pragmatist had won. The law of God was destroyed. What were virtues in themselves had become sin because they were removed from their proper place under the law of God.

The Man of Anti-Law

When Absalom returned, David ordered him to his own house and did not go to see him. Sort of a halfway measure. Since Joab had previously made arrangements for Absalom, Absalom called on him again: "Joab, come here and talk with me about this. Let's work out a little deal." Joab knew what Absalom wanted, though, so he did not go. Absalom, therefore, had his servants set Joab's grain field afire. When all the grain was burning, Joab went running to Absalom, exclaiming, "Absalom, what in the world did you do that for?" Absalom answered, "I knew how to get you here to talk with me" (2 Sam. 14:29-32).

Funny? Yes, in a way it is humorous when we read it. Joab running off to see Absalom! But do you know what else it is? It is anti-law. Absalom was destroying God's

137

law. We have here Absalom the *rebel*! Kill one man, burn another man's fields, rebel against your father with armed force and deception—it is all lawlessness.

Absalom's subsequent revolt against David does not surprise us, nor does it surprise us that he did it in the nastiest way one could imagine. He said nice things to all the people, kissed them and won their hearts away from his father. When he thought he had enough armament as well as enough popular support, he was perfectly willing to see his father killed.

Nathan had prophesied to David, "Thus saith the LORD, Behold, I will raise up evil against thee out of thine own house, and I will take thy wives before thine eyes, and give them unto thy neighbour, and he shall lie with thy wives in the sight of this sun" (2 Sam. 12:11). And this was fulfilled when Absalom, having driven his father out of Jerusalem, "went in unto his father's concubines in the sight of all Israel" (2 Sam. 16:22). He did this publicly so that everyone would know that the breach between him and his father was irreconcilable. No one would bother to work to bring them together; everyone would cast his lot with one or the other.

Absalom was a man of anti-law in the same spirit as the coming Antichrist. The book of Judges says that when there was no king in Israel every man did what was right in his own eyes. Here there is a king, but David had turned his back upon the law of God, and Absalom was in exactly the same place. He was doing what was right in his own eyes. There might as well have been no king at all. David had negated himself as the law giver by turning away from the law of God.

Later, of course, came Absalom's defeat, to which David made this remarkable response:

O my son Absalom, my son, my son Absalom! Would God I had died for thee, O Absalom, my son, my son! And it was told Joab, Behold, the king weepeth and

138

mourneth for Absalom. And the victory that day was turned into mourning unto all the people: for the people heard say that day how the king was grieved for his son. (2 Sam. 18:33b—19:2)
You say, wasn't that beautiful? No, it was not totally beautiful any more. It was a mixed situation. It was beautiful, in a way, because David was still a forgiving man, but we should cry, too, because David the gentle man had become the distributor of lawlessness. Absalom was now not only his son but a criminal—a rebel not only against the constitution of the land but against the law of God. He was a sinner who cared neither for his human father nor God in heaven. Because the law had been destroyed, the people no longer had guidelines, and those who had done right now felt ashamed and guilty: "And the people gat them by stealth that day into the city, as people being ashamed steal away when they flee in battle" (2 Sam. 19:3).

Joab came to David, and, though he may have been acting from a wrong motive, his statement to David was correct. He said, in effect, "David, you're wrong. Get out there and give the people heart. And give them guidelines again." So the king went out and the kingdom continued.

However, because a misplaced love had produced the death of the law of God, lawlessness continued to boil:

And Joab said to Amasa, Art thou in health, my brother? And Joab took Amasa by the beard with the right hand to kiss him. But Amasa took no heed to the sword that was in Joab's hand: so he smote him therewith in the fifth rib, and shed out his bowels to the ground, and struck him not again; and he died. So Joab and Abishai his brother pursued after Sheba the son of Bichri. (2 Sam. 20:9-10)

Lawlessness was loose in the land—boiling, fomenting on every side, ugly, nasty. No mixture here—only murder, intrigue, anything for power. David had brought the situation to this place.

Both observation and the teaching of the Word of God are clear: In the family, church or state when we let the pendulum swing to the place where the absolute law of God is set aside, then that which is good when it is within the circle of God's law becomes not only sin but destructive in the history that flows from it. David did not avenge himself in personal matters, and this was good, but neither did he bring his society the health that comes from applying the law of God.

IX

Elijah and Elisha

To set the stage for Elijah and Elisha we need to review some Jewish history. Solomon's kingdom was divided after his death in 931 B.C. Rehoboam his son remained the ruler of the smaller southern kingdom, while Jereboam, who had fomented rebellion even in Solomon's time, led a revolt which established a new kingdom in the north (1 Kings 12). The northern kingdom was called Israel and the southern kingdom Judah. Later a general named Omri became king of Israel, and then his son Ahab succeeded him. During Ahab's reign, Elijah came on the scene (1 Kings 17).

Elijah ministered during a period of great political activity and change. Assyria's cruel power was growing, and Israel was playing an important role in political events. What Israel was doing was not unknown to the rest of the world. For example, King Ahab and some allies fought the Assyrians to a standstill at Qarqar; and the inscription on the Moabite stone, which dates to that era (c. 830 B.C.) gives a parallel version of political events given in the Bible in 2 Kings 3, making a fascinating connection between biblical and secular history.

Of Elijah himself Young's Concordance says, "Elijah was the grandest and most romantic character Israel ever produced." In the New Testament his name is mentioned more than thirty times, and always in a place of importance. Some of the people who first heard Christ thought that perhaps he was Elijah (Mt. 16:14), which shows that the memory of the prophet was still bright in the minds of the Jews even after 900 years. Elijah was with Moses and Christ on the Mount of Transfiguration (Mt. 17:3). The disciples referred to him when they asked Jesus, "Wilt thou that we command fire to come down from heaven and consume these people?" (Lk. 9:54). When Jesus cried out on the cross the crowd said, "Let us see whether Elijah will come to save him" (Mt. 27:49). And I personally think that Elijah is one of the two great witnesses who will come in the end times (Rev. 11:3-12).

Let us scrutinize the ministry of this man of God and then examine the work of Elisha, the person who both served and succeeded him.

Elijah's Story

Elijah lived a colorful life before the great of the world; he was always in the center of the action. In an incident typical of his entire story, Elijah began his ministry before Ahab the king: "And Elijah the Tishbite, who was of the inhabitants of Gilead, said unto Ahab, As the LORD God of Israel liveth, before whom I stand, there shall not be dew nor rain these years, but according to my word" (1 Kings 17:1).

After making this statement, he fled to a brook where ravens fed him, and after the brook dried up, he went to Zarephath. There a widow took care of him, and "the barrel of meal wasted not, neither did the cruse of oil fail" (1 Kings 17:16). When the widow's son died, Elijah raised him from the dead.

At the end of three years, God ordered him back to what was to become his accustomed place: confronting the great. He again stood face to face with Ahab, who was not some insignificant tribal head but an important Israelite king who stood in the midst of the world's great affairs. Though God saw this man as a sinner and a destroyer, from the secular viewpoint Ahab was a man of stature. And Ahab challenged God's prophet, "Art thou he that troubleth Israel?" Without blinking, Elijah replied, "I have not troubled Israel; but thou, and thy father's house, in that ye have forsaken the commandments of the LORD, and hast followed Baalim" (1 Kings 18: 17-18).

Events swept on to a tremendous public spectacle on Mount Carmel, a situation utterly unique. It was as though the prophet were in a large amphitheatre with television cameras focused on him and a total sociological, religious and intellectual consensus confronting him. The tension grew as the eyes of a whole nation watched him stand alone and challenge the 450 prophets of Baal. "Then the fire of the LORD fell, and consumed the burnt sacrifice, and the wood, and the stones and the dust, and licked up the water that was in the trench. And when all the people saw it, they fell on their faces; and they said, the LORD, he is God; the LORD, he is God" (1 Kings 18:38-39). The fire falling from heaven, false prophets being slain and rain coming at Elijah's command after three years of drought were totally spectacular.

But after this extraordinary moment, Elijah literally had to run for his life because Jezebel, Ahab's queen, threatened it. Jezebel, like her husband, was no minor ruler: She was used to playing her part in world events.

When this one man threatened her religion, status and power, she was furious. Jezebel sent a messenger to Elijah saying, "So let the gods do to me, and more also, if I make not thy life as the life of one of them [the slain prophets of Baal] by tomorrow about this time" (1 Kings 19:2). So Elijah ran for his life.

Elijah, like any other man, became exhausted, and an angel came to help him. And with Elijah this is not at all surprising. In fact, we would expect something like this to happen to him!

Soon afterward God told Elijah, "Elisha the son of Shaphat of Abelmeholah shalt thou anoint to be prophet in thy place" (1 Kings 19:16). So Elijah "departed thence, and found Elisha the son of Shaphat, who was plowing with twelve yoke of oxen before him, and he with the twelfth: and Elijah passed by him, and cast his mantle upon him" (1 Kings 19:19). Just as the incident with Ahab where Elijah is introduced typifies Elijah's ministry, so this scene typifies the ministry of Elisha. We first see Elijah confronting the powerful; we first see Elisha plodding behind a team of oxen.

Although his mantle had been cast upon Elisha, Elijah's ministry was not yet complete. We know of two other important events. The first, the tragedy of Naboth's vineyard (in 1 Kings 21), makes us wrestle with the problem of totalitarian structures. This is important to us for we see a drift toward authoritative government in all of our countries in our own day. Naboth owned a vineyard and wanted to keep it, and all the old customs commanded by God were on his side. But power in the persons of Ahab and Jezebel opposed him. "Why shouldn't Ahab have that property?" Jezebel asked. So she had Naboth murdered.

Suddenly Elijah came on the scene, once more confronting the powerful. Not surprisingly Ahab's first words to the prophet were, "Hast thou found me, O mine enemy?" to which Elijah responded by saying, "I have found thee: because thou hast sold thyself to work evil in the sight of the LORD" (1 Kings 21:20). He then went on to give a prophecy about the terrible fate coming to Ahab and his wife (vv. 20-24). Ahab had been able to stand before the great Assyrian empire, but he could not prevail before Elijah. As we study Elijah's life we come to expect God to use him in such situations. He is the man to challenge a totalitarian structure.

The second event is Elijah's confrontation with Ahaziah, Ahab's son and successor. Ahaziah had fallen through a lattice from a high place and was ill, so he sent messengers to inquire of "Baal-zebub, the god of Ekron." As they were on their way, they, too, were confronted by Elijah. Elijah demanded, "Is it not because there is not a God in Israel, that ye go to enquire of Baalzebub the god of Ekron? Now therefore thus saith the LORD, Thou shalt not come down from that bed on which thou art gone up, but shalt surely die" (2 Kings 1:2-4).

When Ahaziah was given this message, he did what such a king would naturally do: He sent fifty soldiers with their captain to arrest the man who opposed him. Here again power was set against the man of God in an open arena. Fire came down from heaven and destroyed all fifty men and the captain. Later a second fifty came out and the same thing occurred. (This, by the way, is what the disciples were referring to when they asked if they should call down fire from heaven.) A third set of fifty came out, but this time their captain's humility saved them. Elijah returned with them to tell the king he was going to die; and the king did die. In each place Elijah stands at a place of importance in the eyes of men.

At this same time we have given to us one of the few descriptions of the physical appearance of one of the Bible characters. Elijah is called a "hairy man, and girt with a girdle of leather about his loins" (2 Kings 1:8).

At the end of Elijah's time on earth (his *first* time, I would say), he came to the Jordan River and divided the waters by striking them with his mantle. After he had crossed over, he turned to Elisha, who had been his faithful servant for a long time, and said, "Ask what I shall do for thee, before I be taken away from thee." To which Elisha gave this remarkable answer: "I pray thee, let a double portion of thy spirit be upon me" (2 Kings 2:9). I do not think Elisha was asking for *more* than Elijah had. Rather, I think "double portion" is like the French word *double*, meaning a carbon copy or twin. Elisha, I believe, was saying to Elijah, "I want what you have had."

As Elijah was taken up to heaven in the chariot of fire, his mantle fell to the earth, and it is entirely fitting to the structure of this history that Elisha went and picked it up; he was to wear Elijah's mantle. "And he took the mantle of Elijah that fell from him, and smote the waters, and said, Where is the LORD God of Elijah?" (2 Kings 2:14). Our attention naturally is fixed on the miracle of the waters rolling back, but let us also notice his question "Where is the LORD God of Elijah?" Elisha took Elijah's cloak which had fallen from him and it is Elijah's cloak which was used to roll back the waters.

Elijah's departure did not really end his story. When King Jehu later killed Jezebel, he quoted Elijah's prophecy about her death (2 Kings 9:36). A prophecy Elijah had written against the king of Judah was not delivered until after Elijah had left the earth (2 Chron. 21: 12-15). So even after his departure, Elijah remained in the same position—in the midst of great events, confronting the powerful. From his first statement to Ahab to his posthumous prophecy, there was a continuity in Elijah's ministry.

Elisha's Ministry

The first use Elisha made of the power he had received, after the parting of the Jordan, was the "healing" of a spring of water.

And the men of the city said unto Elisha, Behold, I pray thee, the situation of this city is pleasant, as my lord seeth: but the water is naught, and the ground barren. And he said, Bring me a new cruse, and put salt therein. And they brought it to him. And he went forth unto the spring of the waters, and cast the salt in there, and said, Thus saith the LORD, I have healed these waters; there shall not be from thence any more death or barren land. So the waters were healed unto this day, according to the saying of Elisha which he spake. (2 Kings 2:19-22)

This incident conveys the tone of Elisha's work. Elisha did not do something spectacular such as Elijah did on Carmel, nor was he face to face with a great personage. He merely cured a spring of water. The fire on Carmel versus a spring in Jericho. What a contrast! No wonder, then, that in the New Testament times Elisha was not so well remembered as Elijah. There are no quotations in the New Testament concerning Elisha; there are thirty which concern Elijah.

Elisha came to more prominence when he spoke courageously to Jehoram, the king of Israel, but even in this situation there was a difference. Elisha was described by the king's servant as "the son of Shaphat, which poured water on the hands of Elijah" (2 Kings 3:11). Who is this man? the king asked. He is a prophet who was the servant of Elijah, came the reply. Pouring water on someone's hands, like Jesus washing the disciples' feet, was a picture of a servant. Even his identification is linked to a menial task and to his position as servant of his famous predecessor.

The book of 2 Kings goes on to relate other incidents

in Elisha's ministry. He increased a widow's supply of oil, which saved her children from being sold into slavery. He brought back to life the child of a Shunammite woman who had shown kindness by building him a small room to stay in when he was in that area. His inhabiting his "prophet's chamber" is a quiet note—unlike any we find in the life of Elijah.

In another intriguing incident the cry went up, "There is death in the pot" (2 Kings 4:40). Somebody had mistakenly dumped poison gourds into a pot of food, so hungry people were left with nothing to eat. Elisha took some meal, threw it in and then "there was no harm in the pot" (2 Kings 4:41). In another incident involving food, he fed one hundred men with a small amount of barley loaves and corn.

At another time he told Naaman, captain of the armies of Syria, to wash seven times in the Jordan to cure his leprosy. Later someone lost an axe head in the river. Iron axes were not so easy to come by then as now, and the person who had borrowed the axe was in trouble. So Elisha helped him by making the axe head float to the surface. It is typical of Elisha's ministry that he would be dealing with an axe head.

Subsequent events placed Elisha in a place of somewhat greater prominence. Through his prayer, God blinded some Syrian troops who were warring against Israel (2 Kings 6:18). Through his prophecy, given to a messenger from the king, Ben-hadad, king of Syria, abandoned a seige of the city of Samaria (2 Kings 7:1). His prophecy that Hazael would become king of Syria changed the course of that nation (2 Kings 8:11-15). His ordering one of the younger prophets to anoint Jehu king of Israel had similar results in Israel (2 Kings 9:1-26).

In these events Elisha seemed to be in the center of the action. But two things should be noticed. One is the roundabout way in which Elisha often operated. When

150

Elijah confronted power, he did it directly, nakedly. Elisha, however, frequently communicated his messages indirectly through messengers. Second, even then Elisha himself often was an intermediary, for he was carrying out God's commands to Elijah. God had ordered Elijah to "anoint Hazael to be king over Syria: And Jehu the son of Nimshi shalt thou anoint to be king over Israel" (1 Kings 19:15-16). Long after Elijah had been taken to heaven, then, Elisha carried out these commands in his circuitous way. So even though Elisha was in the center of things, he was still, in a very real sense, pouring water on Elijah's hands.

The last thing we are told about Elisha is that after his death a dead man was lowered into Elisha's tomb, and when he touched the prophet's bones, he came back to life (2 Kings 13:20-21). It is typical of Elisha's work that we do not even know the man's name.

151

Elijah and Elisha Compared

As we compare the ministries of these two men, we must remember that Elisha had a "double portion," a carbon copy, of Elijah's spirit. But he had an entirely different ministry. Elijah was before the great of the earth constantly, Elisha only occasionally. And even then, Elisha was overshadowed by Elijah. The phrase "he poured water on his hands" pictures the whole situation. At the beginning of his ministry Elisha used Elijah's mantle to roll back the waters. At the end of his life, he was still fulfilling commands God had spoken to Elijah.

Elisha's ministry, therefore, was a quieter ministry, involving much more care of common people and the common things of life. Was it more or less important than Elijah's? Elisha was in a place more like that of most of us. And all his life he must have been cognizant of Elijah's more eminent place. He was overshadowed by

Elijah both in his lifetime and in the memory of men. As we look at it from a viewpoint hundreds of years later, we might tend to say that Elijah's ministry was greater. But those who drank the healed waters at Jericho, the widow whose children were saved from slavery, those who ate the food from the pot when they were very hungry, Naaman cured of his leprosy, the poor man who had borrowed an axe and would have been ruined by its loss, the man raised from the dead in Elisha's sepulcher who is unnamed to us but eminently important to himself as a man, and many others would surely have thanked God that there was an Elisha as well as an Elijah.

For each of us as Christians, the important thing is that there are some people, whether great or small, who can be thankful that we have lived and that God has worked through us.

X

The
Three Men
in the
Fiery
Furnace

During the reign of Jehoiakim, king of Judah, Nebuchadnezzar, king of Babylon, came against Jerusalem and defeated it, taking both tribute and hostages back to Babylon. The book of Daniel records that some of the vessels of God's house in Jerusalem were placed in the treasure house of Nebuchadnezzar's god: "And the Lord gave Jehoiakim king of Judah into his hand, with part of the vessels of the house of God: which he carried into the land of Shinar to the house of his god: and he brought the vessels into the treasure house of his god" (Dan. 1:2). What this passage portrays, then, as do many others in the Old Testament, is that the struggle is not just that of one nation against another, but the battle between the true God and a false god.

To the extent that the Jews remained faithful to the God of Abraham, Isaac and Jacob, and to the laws of Moses and the revelation of God, there was a tension, a struggle between the true God and false ones. As the

Jews turned away from God and came to a place of unbelief, they ceased to be the covenant people in a religious way, though they continued to be so in a natural, national way. Therefore, God gave them into the hands of their enemies, who took the things of God into their false temples.

Notice also in Daniel 1:2 that Nebuchadnezzar took only part of the temple vessels. Jerusalem was not dismantled all at once; the Chaldean king overcame it gradually, in three great waves of assault, finally burning everything down. The assault described in Daniel 1 was only the first. This means that while the action in the early chapters of Daniel is occurring, life is continuing on in Jerusalem.

One of the most important things happening in Jerusalem during this time was that Jeremiah was there prophesying away. He was saying to the Jews, "Don't you understand you've revolted against the living God, and your rebellion is bearing its natural fruit. Because the living God is a God of steadfast holiness and love, he must punish you." Jeremiah continued his proclamation for a number of years, and then, after Jerusalem was completely demolished, he was dragged away into Egypt. There, according to tradition (the Bible is silent), he died a terrible death. When the book of Hebrews speaks of men who "were sawn asunder" (Heb. 11:37), it may well be speaking of Jeremiah's death, for Jewish tradition says that in Egypt Jeremiah was put into a hollow tree and sawed in two.

This, then, is the historical setting of the first chapters of Daniel.

The Four Young Men
Among the hostages taken from Babylon were four young men:
And the king spake unto Ashpenaz the master of his

eunuchs, that he should bring certain of the children of Israel, and of the king's seed, and of the princes; Children in whom was no blemish, but well favoured, and skilful in all wisdom, and cunning in knowledge, and understanding science, and such as had ability in them to stand in the king's palace, and whom they might teach the learning and the tongue of the Chaldeans. And the king appointed them a daily provision of the king's meat, and of the wine which he drank: so nourishing them three years, that at the end thereof they might stand before the king. Now among these were of the children of Judah, Daniel, Hananiah, Mishael, and Azariah: Unto whom the prince of the eunuchs gave names: for he gave unto Daniel the name of Belteshazzar; and to Hananiah, of Shadrach; and to Mishael, of Meshach; and to Azariah, of Abednego. (Dan. 1:3-7)

These young men were given Chaldean names—Belteshazzar, Shadrach, Meshach and Abed-nego—and put through a special kind of test to see if they were worthy of responsibility in the king's palace.

The narrative continues with a statement that is important to the entire story: "But Daniel purposed in his heart that he would not defile himself with the portion of the king's food, nor with the wine which he drank: therefore he requested of the prince of the eunuchs that he might not defile himself" (Dan. 1:8). Daniel must have refused for one of two reasons, either because he thought the palace food would destroy his health or because it was somehow connected with idol worship, but we are not told. Whatever the reason, for three years all four of these young men had the courage not to compromise.

The situation in a way seems unimportant—it dealt only with food. Nevertheless, the men's response showed a set of mind which will be manifested throughout their history. These were men of standards. In even lesser things they stood courageously and did not compromise.

We appreciate the courage of Daniel and his friends even more when we realize how much they were jeopardizing. They had a great future ahead of them, for the Chaldeans perceived them to be men with special gifts. Verse 4 shows they were what we might call today "first-class people"—skillful in wisdom, endowed with knowledge, brilliant in learning, able to stand in the king's palace. And they had more than natural gifts, for God gave them special ones: "As for these four children, God gave them knowledge and skill in all learning and wisdom: and Daniel had understanding in all visions and dreams" (Dan. 1:17).

Because of their natural gifts and the gifts they received directly from the hand of God, they were men who could expect to have an increasing influence at the court. They were not people who had nothing to jeopardize.

And their future was not in some backward village but in the tremendous empire of Nebuchadnezzar when Babylon was queen of the world. Babylon was the center of culture, the center of power, the center of prestige, the center of influence. And these four gifted young men, already in a place of importance, had a great future in front of them. After Daniel and his three friends had passed the test and demonstrated their quality to the king, their potential prestige rose even higher: "And the king communed with them; and among them all was found none like Daniel, Hananiah, Mishael, and Azariah: therefore stood they before the king. And in all matters of wisdom and understanding, that the king enquired of them, he found them ten times better than all the magicians and astrologers that were in all his realm" (Dan. 1:19-20).

158

Nebuchadnezzar's Dream

The second chapter of Daniel describes events at about the time of the fall of Jerusalem (in 587 or 586 B.C.). Around the time when the third wave of assault destroyed Jerusalem, Nebuchadnezzar dreamed a dream, but—a slight complication—he forgot what the dream was about. A small but important difficulty! He called his astrologers and said, "You have two tasks and not one. First tell me what the dream was and then interpret it." Now, had he told them the dream, undoubtedly they would have fished around for some interpretation, but having to find out first what the dream was, they were really in trouble.

When the wise men told the king, "This is too much to ask," the king replied, "Then I'm going to kill the lot of you—because it's quite obvious you are frauds."

This slaughter would have included Daniel, Shadrach, Meshach and Abed-nego, who were now listed among Nebuchadnezzar's wise men. Daniel's response was to turn to prayer. He immediately informed his three friends of the dilemma and asked "that they would desire mercies of the God of heaven concerning this secret" (Dan. 2:18). So the four young men went to prayer in heathen Babylon. Personal jeopardy was involved in their situation but, more importantly, so was the glory of God. That the first reaction of these men was to pray shows again the kind of men they were.

In this case God revealed the dream to Daniel in a vision and then gave him its interpretation, and immediately Daniel was faced with a choice. We could imagine him jumping up, running down to the court and boasting, "Here I am. I am the man who can do what all the astrologers cannot do." That would have placed him ahead of all the other wise men, who, as we know from archaeological discoveries, comprised a most powerful class in ancient Babylon. But instead of doing that, he

159

again demonstrated the quality of his character. His first reaction was not to run anywhere and tell anybody. The first thing he did was to praise God, to thank him for the answered prayer. In a paean of praise, Daniel exclaimed:

Blessed be the name of God for ever and ever: for wisdom and might are his: And he changeth the times and the seasons: he removeth kings, and setteth up kings; he giveth wisdom unto the wise, and knowledge to them that know understanding: He revealeth the deep and secret things: he knoweth what is in the darkness, and the light dwelleth with him. I thank thee, and praise thee, O thou God of my fathers, who hast given me wisdom and might, and hast made known unto me now what we desired of thee: for thou hast now made known unto us the king's matter. (Dan. 2:20-23)

160

Daniel in the Presence of the King

It is one thing to thank God privately for a specific answer to prayer, but what would Daniel say in the presence of the king? Would he be a different man in the presence of the great Nebuchadnezzar than in his own room and among his friends? He had an opportunity to acquire tremendous prestige and advance his professional life. He was a man of gifts and abilities who now had the opportunity of receiving praise from the ruler of the then-known world.

Yet as he stood in the presence of the pagan king Nebuchadnezzar, Daniel's first statement was much like what he prayed alone. He kept the king waiting to hear the dream and the interpretation until he had given praise to God. "There is a God in heaven that revealeth secrets," he told the king (Dan. 2:28).

Throughout the Jews' captivity in Babylon, the phrase *the God of heaven* apparently was the main designation used for the living God, and it contrasted him with all other gods. He is not a god who is stuck in a temple or a god of one nation. He cannot be limited. He is the God of all the heavens, the God of the universe, the Creator.

We must remember that Daniel's using this term was an affront to Nebuchadnezzar because Daniel was saying in effect, "You have overcome Jerusalem, but the God of heaven, the God that the Jews worship, is a greater God than your god, O Nebuchadnezzar." It took great courage to make this speech.

And having so much opportunity for personal aggrandizement, Daniel discounted his own cleverness. "But as for me, this secret is not revealed to me for any wisdom that I have more than any living..." (Dan. 2:30); in other words, "The understanding did not come because I am wise and clever, but because the God of heaven, who is a living God, revealed it to me." One of the big dangers and temptations in Christianity today is 161 to be infiltrated with the cult of cleverness, but Daniel carefully removed the praise from himself and placed it upon God.

We now see clearly the answer to our earlier question. Daniel's first action, not only when he was alone but also when he was in the presence of the king and the surrounding culture, was to praise God.

Daniel's success in interpreting the dream gave him and his three friends a greater future than ever, for "then the king made Daniel a great man, and gave him many great gifts, and made him ruler over the whole province of Babylon, and chief of the governors over all the wise men of Babylon. Then Daniel requested of the king, and he set Shadrach, Meshach, and Abed-nego, over the affairs of the province of Babylon: but Daniel sat in the gate of the king" (Dan. 2:48-49). The "gate of the king" was the highest place in the country, the place where judgment was meted out. Daniel was now the great one.

And Shadrach, Meshach and Abed-nego had also come to a great place.

Our generation uses a term I dislike very much, but I am going to use it anyway. It is the term a "comer." A "comer" is a man who, because of his gifts, you can be sure is going to be a great fellow in the future. You can be certain he is really going to do something. The term bothers me because of the cult of cleverness which I have mentioned, but if the term were ever appropriate it would be here. These Jewish men were "comers." They had the future before them. Having natural ability and special spiritual gifts, standing before Nebuchadnezzar, the arbitrator of the world of power, and in the midst of the world culture, they were the men of the future.

Nebuchadnezzar's Image

162 Some time after Daniel had solved the problem of Nebuchadnezzar's dream, Nebuchadnezzar made an image of gold, ninety feet in height and nine feet in breadth, and set it up on the plain of Dura for the people to adore.

Nebuchadnezzar the king made an image of gold, whose height was threescore cubits, and the breadth thereof six cubits: he set it up in the plain of Dura, in the province of Babylon. Then Nebuchadnezzar the king sent to gather together the princes, the governors, and the captains, the judges, the treasurers, the counsellors, the sheriffs, and all the rulers of the provinces, to come to the dedication of the image which Nebuchadnezzar the king had set up. Then the princes, the governors, and captains, the judges, the treasurers, the counsellors, the sheriffs, and all the rulers of the provinces, were gathered together unto the dedication of the image that Nebuchadnezzar the king had set up; and they stood before the image that

Nebuchadnezzar had set up. Then an herald cried aloud, To you it is commanded, O people, nations, and languages, That at what time ye hear the sound of the cornet, flute, harp, sackbut, psaltery, dulcimer, and all kinds of music, ye fall down and worship the golden image that Nebuchadnezzar the king hath set up: And whoso falleth not down and worshippeth shall the same hour be cast into the midst of a burning fiery furnace. Therefore at that time, when all the people heard the sound of the cornet, flute, harp, sackbut, psaltery, and all kinds of music, all the people, the nations, and the languages, fell down and worshipped the golden image that Nebuchadnezzar the king had set up. (Dan. 3:1-7)

But there was a slight problem. Three men did not fall down and worship. These three men were the three young men who had such a promising future. Where was Daniel? We do not know, though it has often been discussed. We can be sure he did not bow; that would not fit in with the rest of the story. Perhaps he was away someplace on the king's business.

So the Babylonian eyes were fastened on Shadrach, Meshach and Abed-nego. In a way, it is good for us that this incident did not involve Daniel. Daniel seems like such a tremendous character, superior to us. But here were three lesser characters standing in a threatening situation. And these three young men did not bow.

Immediately some people, who were probably jealous already, came running up to Nebuchadnezzar, exclaiming: "There are certain Jews whom thou hast set over the affairs of the province of Babylon, Shadrach, Meshach, and Abed-nego; these men, O king, have not regarded thee: they serve not thy gods, nor worship the golden image which thou hast set up" (Dan. 3:12). Notice this matter of the gods against God again. This is not a clash merely of one culture against another, or one peo-

163

ple against another—it is the true God versus the false gods.

Naturally, Nebuchadnezzar was used to getting his own way, especially in such a crucial situation as this. So you can imagine his reaction: He was furious. And in his rage he commanded Shadrach, Meshach and Abed-nego to be brought before the furnace.

As Nebuchadnezzar confronted the three men, he asked them:

> Is it true, O Shadrach, Meshach, and Abed-nego, do not ye serve my gods, nor worship the golden image which I have set up? Now if ye be ready that at what time ye hear the sound of the cornet, flute, harp, sackbut, psaltery, and dulcimer, and all kinds of music, ye fall down and worship the image which I have made; well: but if ye worship not, ye shall be cast the same hour into the midst of a burning fiery furnace; and *who is that God that shall deliver you out of my hands?* (Dan. 3:14-15)

164

As these three young men stood against a total culture, the accepted consensus of their day, they made a reply that is the crucial statement for our study: "O Nebuchadnezzar, we are not careful to answer thee in this matter. If it be so, our God whom we serve is able to deliver us from the burning fiery furnace, and he will deliver us out of thine hand, O king. But if not, be it known unto thee, O king, that we will not serve thy gods, nor worship the golden image which thou hast set up" (Dan. 3:16-18).

The three men thus said several astonishing things in this speech. First, they stated that while human wisdom would suggest they give the king a careful answer, hedging it so that it did not offend, they instead were going to give a completely straightforward answer. Expediency was set aside. Second, they directly contradicted the implication of Nebuchadnezzar's question, "Who is that God that shall deliver you out of my hands?" They affirmed to the king that this discussion did not turn upon *whether* God exists or on *whether* he is able to rescue them. "That just isn't the topic of conversation, Nebuchadnezzar," they implied. "God is able. He does exist. He's different from your gods who have to be carried around by men; he is the living God, the God of heaven, the God of power in Babylon as much as in Judea. He is a real God. The point is not whether he is able to deliver, because he is able. If he wills to deliver, he can deliver."

And finally, and most marvelous of all, they declared that whether God did or did not deliver them, they were not going to worship the image. Their message was plain: "If God does deliver, we won't worship. If God doesn't deliver, we still won't worship."

Two Possible Outcomes

165

Immediately, we can see that this situation will have one of two outcomes. God will either rescue these men or not rescue them. We see an instance later in the book of Daniel when God did deliver. Daniel had been in a lion's den all night, and the king (Darius at that time) came to the lion's den early in the morning and called with a lamentable voice: "O Daniel, servant of the living God, is thy God, whom thou servest continually, able to deliver thee from the lions?" (Dan. 6:20). It is interesting to note the exact parallel between this question and the one Nebuchadnezzar years before had asked the three young men. In the case of Daniel in the lion's den, God had delivered; Daniel was safe.

Hebrews 11, a chapter about faith, recounts many times when God did rescue faithful men and women. After mentioning the faith of Moses, Rahab and other Old Testament characters, the chapter speaks of people "who through faith subdued kingdoms, wrought righteousness, obtained promises, stopped the mouths of lions [undoubtedly this refers to Daniel], quenched the violence of fire, escaped the edge of the sword, out of weakness were made strong, waxed valiant in fight, turned to flight the armies of the aliens. Women received their dead raised to life again ..." (Heb. 11: 33-35). But notice that this text about faith goes on without a break to point out that sometimes the God who is able to deliver does not deliver:

Others were tortured, not accepting deliverance; that they might obtain a better resurrection: And others had trial of cruel mockings and scourgings, yea, moreover of bonds and imprisonment: They were stoned, they were sawn asunder, were tempted, were slain with the sword: they wandered about in sheepskins and goatskins; being destitute, afflicted, tormented; (Of whom the world was not worthy:) they wandered in deserts, and in mountains, and in dens and caves of the earth. (Heb. 11:35-38)

And yet these people were also walking in the way of faith.

So the book of Hebrews portrays exactly what the three friends said as they confronted Nebuchadnezzar, namely, there are two kinds of times, two kinds of situations. Sometimes the One who is able to deliver does deliver, and sometimes he does not. The apostle Paul, for instance, experienced both kinds: Sometimes he was saved from suffering, sometimes he was not.

But the thing to notice very carefully in Hebrews 11 is that whether the people were delivered or not delivered, the people named stood in these situations in a position of faith toward either outcome. Many times both situations will occur in one man's lifetime, as in the case of Paul.

In our focal story in the book of Daniel, Shadrach, Meshach and Abed-nego, who may already have heard that

Jeremiah had been sawed in half in Egypt, expressed their faith in God regardless of what the outcome of their situation would be. "Whether God delivers us or does not deliver us doesn't change anything," they told the king, "we still aren't going to bow."

The lesson in Daniel 3 is practical, because life is like that. Sometimes Christians are delivered and sometimes they are not. And here we face the realities involving the entire movement of history, the struggle in the heavenlies as well as in the seen world. The man of faith can glorify God. The man of faith does not bow.

The Fiery Furnace

Nebuchadnezzar, as we have seen, was in a blind fury, so he commanded that the furnace be made seven times hotter than it had ever been before. And then he had Shadrach, Meshach and Abed-nego thrown in.

Then Nebuchadnezzar the king was astonied, and rose up in haste, and spake, and said unto his counsellors, Did not we cast three men bound into the midst of the fire? They answered and said unto the king, True, O king. He answered and said, Lo, I see four men loose, walking in the midst of the fire, and they have no hurt; and the form of the fourth is like the Son of God. (Dan 3:24-25)

It is true that the Hebrew phrase which the Authorized Version translates "like the Son of God" is literally "a son of the gods." But I think the King James translators had a good reason for their rendering. Remembering that 1 Corinthians 10:1-4 expressly states that Christ was with Moses in the wilderness, we should not be surprised if it were Christ, the second Person of the Trinity, who was in the midst of the fiery furnace. At any rate, whether or not the translation should be "a son of the gods" makes no difference because it was Nebuchadnezzar who was speaking and he was not in a position to know. A few moments after this first statement, he also called the fourth person in the fire an "angel" (v. 28).

Another thing which Nebuchadnezzar observed in the fire was that although the men had been bound and cast into the furnace, they were now loose. And they were no longer alone, or, to use a modern term, they were not alienated. They were not lonely. They had someone with them.

One reason that the higher critics hate the book of Daniel and have done so much to try to destroy it is that this event did not occur in some unknown corner of the world but in the midst of the world's great culture. Because it is a testimony to the miraculousness of the wonder of God, many critics would destroy it, if they could, in order to get rid of this witness that God is God and not just a name.

"Then Nebuchadnezzar came near to the mouth of the burning fiery furnace, and spake, and said, Shadrach, Meshach, and Abed-nego, ye servants of the most high God, come forth, and come hither. Then Shadrach, Meshach, and Abed-nego, came forth of the midst of the fire" (Dan. 3:26). This testimony to God's power was witnessed by men who were the leaders of the nation: "And the princes, governors, and captains, and the king's counsellors, being gathered together, saw these men, upon whose bodies the fire had no power, nor was an hair of their head singed, neither were their coats changed, nor the smell of fire had passed on them" (Dan. 3:27). These leaders did not make any existential leap. They saw that the fire had had no power on the bodies of the three young men: It did not singe their hair or change their coat or leave any taint of odor on them. No wonder men who hate the Word of God want to get rid of these passages, for we have here one of the cases where the God who exists and is able to deliver did deliver before witnesses in a most definite way.

But let us remind ourselves again that sometimes God does not deliver. The story of Stephen in Acts 7, for example, stands in contrast to the story of the three men in the fiery furnace. Stephen testified to the leaders of his culture that Jesus was the Messiah prophesied in the Old Testament. And Stephen, as he concluded this testimony, was stoned to death:

When they heard these things, they were cut to the heart, and they gnashed on him with their teeth. But he, being full of the Holy Spirit, looked up stedfastly into heaven, and saw the glory of God, and Jesus standing on the right hand of God. . . . Then they cried out with a loud voice, and stopped their ears, and ran upon him with one accord, And cast him out of the city, and stoned him: and the witnesses laid down their clothes at a young man's feet, whose name was Saul. And they stoned Stephen, calling upon God, and saying, Lord Jesus, receive my spirit. (Acts 7:54-59)

169

Stephen, like the three men in Babylon, is an example of a man of faith, but in his case God did not deliver. In both situations, though, God was glorified.

Another parallel between the story in Acts and the story in Daniel is that in both cases God did not let his people walk alone. He was with them. If I am correct that the fourth person in the fiery furnace was the second Person of the Trinity, then the *same* Person was with Stephen as with the three young men, the Person whom we know after the Incarnation by the name of the Lord Jesus Christ. The One who walked with the men in the furnace was the same One who, having been raised from the dead, having ascended into heaven and having been seated at the right hand of God the Father almighty, when Stephen, a man of faith, died, did not remain seated but stood to welcome him. Men of faith are not alone, not alone in either kind of situation.

The crux of the story of the three young men, as with Stephen, is that they put everything, including their lives, on the line. The text says that Nebuchadnezzar, understanding now the difference between their God and his own, praised God and said, "Blessed be the God of Shadrach, Meshach, and Abed-nego, who hath sent his angel, and delivered his servants that trusted in him, and have changed the king's word, and yielded their bodies, that they might not serve nor worship any god, except their own God" (Dan. 3:28). These men yielded their bodies and refused to serve any god except the living God. The text says they trusted God, whether or not he was going to deliver them.

Being God's Man or Woman Today
In basic things, our day is no different from these earlier times. The lessons in the first three chapters of Daniel hold for us too.

170

First, strong warriors for Jesus Christ, men and women of faith, are not created instantaneously; they do not come forth mechanically; they grow. No man has stood in a great place who has not, by the grace of God, stood in lesser ones before. If a person cannot stand faithful in a lesser place, how will he be able to stand in the center of his own culture in front of the twentieth century's own kind of fiery furnace? To be a man or woman of faith requires training.

Second, if a person does not give glory to God in his lesser accomplishments, crediting God and not exulting in his own cleverness, he will not be able to give glory to God when men begin to praise him for "greater things" God does through him.

Third, having great gifts, both natural and spiritual, does not excuse a person from trusting God. A person with great gifts (a "comer") cannot say, "I have great gifts and a great future, especially in Christian activity;

therefore I can draw back." No. The greater the gifts, the more a person has to lay them gently but definitely at God's feet, whether God chooses to deliver him or not. I conclude with these key verses and charge all of us in the name of the Lord Jesus Christ that confronted by a consensus which is our own fiery furnace in the twentieth century, and facing one of two possible outcomes, we learn to say with reality, by God's grace: "O Nebuchadnezzar, we are not careful to answer thee in this matter. If it be so, our God whom we serve is able to deliver us from the burning fiery furnace, and he will deliver us out of thine hand, O king. But if not, be it known unto thee, O king, that we will not serve thy gods, nor worship the golden image which thou hast set up."

XI

What Difference Has Looking Made? (A Christmas Study)

After the angels had appeared to them, the shepherds of Bethlehem ran down the hill to see the baby they had been told about. They came "with haste." Luke's account in 2:8-18 ties together a glorious opening of the heavens, the speaking or singing of angels and some ordinary shepherds who were simply tending their flocks. The utterly supernatural took place in the framework of their natural habitat, and their reaction was simple and human: "We've heard about this thing; let's go see it." In a profound sense, the act of religious intensity is as natural as any other movement of life. And they went to Bethlehem with haste, obviously because of the reality of the situation which confronted them.

What Are We Looking At?
Let us imagine that we are with the shepherds on those hills in Palestine. We have seen and heard the angels,

and we have begun to run to Bethlehem. We come bursting into the presence of Mary, Joseph and the baby, and immediately we wonder: What are we looking at?

First of all, we are looking at a true baby. He is not an idea or a religious experience. He is a newborn infant who makes noises and cries when he gets hungry. What we are looking at is real, simple, definite, complete. We are looking at a true baby. This observation alone could launch us into a whole study about the modern concepts of Jesus and the kerygma, for it stands against the notion that Jesus exists or becomes something because we preach him or because we worship him.

Second, there is no reason to think that the baby shows any special manifestations. An artist such as Rembrandt can paint him with light emanating from his body and if we understand the light as symbolic, it is safe enough. But if we think of it as more than that, it is harmful. There is no halo about the baby's head. Certainly there is no halo around Mary's head. What we see is a young Jewish mother, probably seventeen or eighteen years old. She may be pretty or she may not be. We see her husband, and we see a little baby who does not show any marks that would distinguish him from any other infant.

Though we cannot observe it, however, there is something very special about this baby: He has been born of a virgin. From the scriptural viewpoint, this is a once-for-all-in-history occurrence. Mary had said to the angel who told her she would become pregnant, "How shall this be, seeing I know not a man?" (Lk. 1:34). The word *virgin* is not to be conceived of any less strictly than this. Translators can do all they want to try to make Isaiah 7:14 speak of a young maid without any connotation of virginity, but one cannot study the Gospels and fail to see that Isaiah's prophecy means exactly this—the baby would have no human father whatsoever; no man would have any part in the birth of this child.

The books that explain sex to little children somewhere along the line mention that a baby must have a father. That certainly is generally true, and it is a nice way to teach our children. But when we come to the point of saying that there *must* be a father, we must make one exception: The infant in the manger is special because he is the one person who has not had a human father. He is virgin-born in this absolute sense.

However, there is something more. Not only does he lack a human father, he has God as his Father. The angel had told Mary, "The Holy Ghost shall come upon thee, and the power of the Highest shall overshadow thee: therefore also that holy thing which shall be born of thee shall be called the Son of God" (Lk. 1:35). We must see, though, that God is his Father not just because God caused him to be born physically by some distinct intervention, but because God has been his Father forever. 175
The little baby we see lying here is the second Person of the Trinity. He himself has been God forever. This baby is God who has taken on flesh. This is what I am looking at!

Why Did He Come?

Now that we know what we are looking at, we must ask the question, Why did God come into this world? Only the scriptural answer will suffice: The second Person of the Trinity has been born because he loves the world.

But why did he come this way, as a little baby? Why did he choose to lie in a manger and be cared for by a human mother, with the sweetness but the utter weakness of a newborn babe? He came this way because he came to meet the central need of men. He did not come to overthrow the Romans, though a lot of the Jews would have loved that. If he had, he would have come riding on a great conquering steed. The *central* reason he came was not to raise the living standards of the world. Surely if twentieth-century man were going to vote on the way he would like a messiah to appear, he would want him loaded down with moneybags from heaven. He did not come primarily to teach and relieve ignorance—perhaps then he would have come laden with books. An angel had revealed to Joseph the primary task for which he came: "Thou shalt call his name JESUS: for he shall save his people from their sins" (Mt. 1:21).

How is Jesus going to fulfill this promise? The fulfillment cannot be separated from Calvary's cross—from the nails, the hammer, the harshness of such a death. Jesus as the Passover Lamb will complete the promise the Jews affirmed in the Passover for fifteen hundred years. He is going to save his people by his act of Passover obedience.

When we perceive the simplicity and yet the grandeur **176** of what is involved, we are overwhelmed. The second Person of the Trinity lies in the manger for a reason. Because he loves the world, he has come not just to eliminate the peripheral results of man's Fall (though these will be totally removed at his second coming); he is here to cut the nerve of man's real dilemma, to solve the problem from which all other problems flow. The "condition of man" is not what modern man thinks it is. Man is a sinner who needs an overwhelming love. Jesus has come to save his people from their sins. This is not to say that he has no interest in these other things now, but we must not get the matters reversed—the central thing is central.

What Are We Going to Do with Him?

What then are we going to do with this Savior of the world? What am *I*, and what are *you*, going to do with him?

Many believed in him when he was still an infant, and

when they did so the baby became their Savior. The shepherds believed, regardless of the simplicity with which they understood: "And the shepherds returned, glorifying and praising God for all the things that they had heard and seen, as it was told unto them" (Lk. 2:20). Though they believed with less understanding than we who have the New Testament, and though we might even think of them as believing within the Old Testament framework as Old Testament saints, they nonetheless did believe, and they will be in heaven with us. They are in the church of Jesus Christ.

But many, I am sure, did not believe. The shepherds must have run into a tremendous dilemma when "they made known abroad the saying which was told them concerning this child" (Lk. 2:17). Luke goes on to tell us that "all they that heard it wondered at those things which were told them by the shepherds" (Lk. 2:18), and we cannot doubt that those who wondered must have been split into two camps. Some believed, while others did not. We know, for example, what Herod did when he heard who had been born! In most cases, though, the response was probably not so extreme. Some would say, "I don't believe it." And some must have shrugged their shoulders: "All right, but I don't need a Savior." I can hardly believe the shepherds spent more than a few hours telling their story without encountering these two negative reactions.

The shepherds, however, were overwhelmed by what they had seen. This moment would be more real to them than their own small hearths to which they returned after taking care of the sheep. So as they moved through the streets of Bethlehem, speaking to people they knew, they must have been amazed to hear someone say, "I don't believe it." Or to meet someone who believed but did not care. These people who heard the shepherds made an eternal decision. Some of them missed their

177

opportunity to be in heaven because they did not believe the shepherds or feel the need for a Savior.

As we ourselves have run down the hill with the shepherds, looked at the baby and heard the shepherds' testimony, have we believed? If we have, that is a happy thing indeed, for it means we are now Christians. That is fine, but then we must ask ourselves: What difference has this looking made in our present lives?

At Christmastime, we set up our Christmas trees and toy trains. We may even walk along singing carols or we may preach a sermon, but these bits and pieces are barren if we are thinking only of them or even only of being in heaven, and are not stopping to ask ourselves, "What difference does it make in my life now?"

What difference *has* looking made? I think we can approach the answer by thinking about the shepherds and looking through the book of Luke. Having had this overwhelming experience in the midst of their normal environment and having believed in the Savior, can we imagine one of the shepherds remarking, "It's very nice that I've seen an angel and it is nice I have seen the Christ, the Messiah the Jews have been waiting for for so long. It's nice that I've believed in him (unlike some of the other people in Bethlehem) and that I'm going to be in heaven. But really, in practice, it's not going to make any difference at all in my life"? This is inconceivable.

Luke tells us that when Jesus chose his disciples four fishermen "forsook all, and followed him" (Lk. 5:11). Also Matthew the tax-gatherer "left all, rose up, and followed him" (Lk. 5:28). Though the shepherds did not have a call to some clearly defined action (their contact with Christ was at a different historic point), their lives must have been changed.

Facing Old Sins

Since the shepherds were much like each one of us, they

faced a round of old sins when they returned to life-as-usual. In the light of their experience of looking at the face of the baby Jesus, in the light of their understanding of that situation, can we imagine them continuing to live in sin as though it were normal, without being sorry and having real repentance? I think not. I would suggest that the shepherds, full of the reality of what they had seen in the heavens and in the manger, would have been sorry for their past sins and even more if they sinned again.

When John the Baptist prepared the way for the preaching of the gospel, he was "preaching the baptism of repentance unto the remission of sins" (Lk. 3:3). When Jesus began his ministry, his message was exactly the same: "Repent: for the kingdom of heaven is at hand" (Mt. 4:17). Repentance is not to be despised—it is part of the Christian message. Everyone needs real repentance. Let us hope we go further and refrain from sin. But we cannot get this far unless we have real sorrow   179
for our past sins.

Facing Ridicule, Hate and Need
We can imagine a shepherd being jeered at by the first man to whom he told his story, but can we imagine the ridicule stopping him? The shepherd might have been brought up short; successive jeers might have worn him down; but surely, because of the objective reality through which he personally had gone, he would not have been silenced.

Such persecution is natural in a world that hates God. Jesus taught during his ministry, "Blessed are ye, when men shall hate you, and when they shall separate you from their company, and shall reproach you, and cast out your name as evil, for the Son of man's sake. Rejoice ye in that day, and leap for joy: for, behold, your reward is great in heaven: for in the like manner did their fathers unto the prophets" (Lk. 6:22-23). This is exactly what we are to expect after we have accepted Jesus as our Lord and Savior—but we are not to quit. As a matter of fact, we are to receive ridicule with quietness (which does not mean we should be unconcerned about the opposition) and rejoice because there is a reward in heaven. We are not to stop telling our story because of the jeering of the consensus that surrounds us and opposes the Christian message.

Similarly, imagine a shepherd coming away from the manger knowing who this baby was. How would he respond to someone who spoke roughly to him? Can we imagine him taking his great big shepherd's fist and smashing the fellow to the ground? "Peace on earth, goodwill toward men," he had just heard the angels say. The angels had not made some long theological statement (though much theology was there). Rather, they had spoken of the final end to this matter now beginning (if we can speak of the manger as a beginning, for these things really began in the councils of eternity). They had proclaimed the peace of Christ which would come to completeness in Christ's millennial reign on the earth and in eternity. So, although his character would not have been totally changed, with this cry ringing in his ears the shepherd could hardly have punched the man in the nose.

Jesus put this down as universal: "But I say unto you which hear, Love your enemies, do good to them which hate you, Bless them that curse you, and pray for them which despitefully use you" (Lk. 6:27-28). We cannot now bring complete peace on the earth. We wait for the coming of our Lord. Our attitude, however, ought to be in this direction. As citizens of God's kingdom, peace on earth, goodwill to men, should be a reality to us. We are to bring this attitude even into a totally opposite situation.

Of course, in our personal relationships we cannot

180

attain perfection. We often find it hard to refrain from fighting back, but in our personal relationships the command of our Lord is not a theory or a pious hope. The angels' message should be an attitude in our heart. Or can we imagine a shepherd coming out from the Savior meeting some fellow in tattered rags who says, "It's time for me to pay you the dollar I owe you. I have it in my pocket, but if I give it to you I can't even buy a crumb." After the wonder of facing the Savior of the world, could the shepherd take his debtor by the throat, push him down, rifle his pockets and send him into the night cold and hungry?

Jesus gave another universal command which relates to this: "Be ye therefore merciful, as your Father also is merciful" (Lk. 6:36). Our standard of mercy is to be the mercy our Father has shown us. The teaching of the baby Jesus when he is grown relates us to the shepherds, and we are commanded always to have the same attitude the shepherds would have had when they came away from the manger. We cannot come away from Jesus' presence and be unmerciful in the practical areas of life.

Sharing and Praying

Let us now imagine one of the shepherds being uprooted and moving to a new locality. Let us say the Romans picked him up and put him on some hills in Asia Minor. Can we imagine him sitting by a small fire surrounded by other shepherds with sheep nosing about and not saying, "Well, men, one night I was sitting like this when..."? He had had a once-in-history experience! Of course he would share it! If he was transplanted to a new country, he would certainly want to convey this message to his new companions.

This is a universal, too. Jesus told a man he had healed, "Return to thine own house, and shew how great things God hath done unto thee. And he went his

181

way, and published throughout the whole city how great things Jesus had done unto him" (Lk. 8:39). This man, after being healed, just went out and talked. The same should be true of each of us, regardless of our location.

As we continue to reflect on the shepherds' experience while we move through the Gospel of Luke, let us consider how seeing and hearing the angels would have affected the shepherds' praying. While the reality of all this was upon the shepherds, I think prayer would have been an exceedingly simple experience. Communication with God would have become easy because they had seen the supernatural. It had not been miles above their heads, as it were. For if the shepherds heard the angels, why shouldn't God now hear the shepherds? If on the night after all this had occurred a shepherd were sitting in the same place where twenty-four hours before 182 he had seen the heavens opened, and if he had a child who was ill, it is inconceivable, even if he had known nothing previously about prayer, that he would not have shouted up to heaven. We can envision him sitting there without knowing much about the realities of prayer—not knowing that he could just pray in his heart —and thinking, "Well, I could hear them. Surely God can hear me."

Because we know that a person can pray in his heart without shouting and still be heard, we can see that this shepherd's situation would be exactly what Luke portrays of Jesus when he describes him "alone praying" (Lk. 9:18). This description indicates the simplicity and centrality of Jesus' communication with God. Doesn't this reveal something often wrong in our own prayer life? Prayer is not to be forced, for God is not far off. When confronted with the reality of God and the commands and promises of God, it is natural for a person to speak.

Being in the Proper Place

Having seen the glory of the heavenly host, could a shepherd any longer think of himself as the center of the universe, expecting all things to get out of *his* way? The glory would have been too overwhelming. A child may feel sure of himself as he schemes his schemes. When he was a little boy, my son used to devise great plans for fighting off the Russians if they were to come up the mountain. And he was totally serious. But if Russian tanks had ever begun to roll up out of the valley, we would know we were going to be overrun. When the force of reality strikes us with all its drive, our own imaginings are seen in their proper perspective. Facing the glory of heaven, the shepherds of Bethlehem surely would not have thought that they could drive their little cart through all the universe, stamping harshly upon God's place.

Christ made it clear that no one is to make himself the 183 center of the universe: "If any man will come after me, let him deny himself, and take up his cross daily, and follow me" (Lk. 9:23). This is a universal.

Likewise, it is difficult to imagine the shepherds quarreling about personal prerogatives. I cannot imagine being faced with the glory of heaven and the Savior of the world and then saying to someone else, "I'm first, fellow. I'm first."

When Jesus' disciples disputed about who should be greatest, Jesus gave another universal. He "took a child, and set him by him, And said unto them, Whosoever shall receive this child in my name receiveth me: and whoever shall receive me receiveth him that sent me: for he that is least among you, the same shall be great" (Lk. 9:47-48). We can see the reasonableness of this universal when we bring it down to a situation we can grasp, like the reaction of the shepherds to the heavenly host.

Rejecting Materialism

After this experience, would the shepherds have accepted materialism as either an adequate philosophy or an adequate practice in life? Wouldn't looking at the glory of heaven readjust one's values? I think so. If the shepherds had been educated men (which they were not), materialism as a philosophy would not now have sounded very attractive! And in practice, an accumulation of gold jingling in the pockets and angels singing in the heavens do not quite fit together. But also as a practice of life—not necessarily money jingling in my pocket but other things jingling in my life—materialism comes short.

Shortly after Jesus was born, Joseph began to practice his trade in Bethlehem and was able to move his family out of the stable into a house by the time the wise men came. But Jesus' experience of poverty did not stop. Jesus could say soberly and honestly during his ministry, "Foxes have holes, and birds of the air have nests; but the Son of man hath nowhere to lay his head" (Lk. 9:58).

Jesus, in didactic teaching, forcefully presented this as a universal:

Take heed, and beware of covetousness: for a man's life consisteth not in the abundance of the things which he possesseth. And he spake a parable unto them, saying, The ground of a certain rich man brought forth plentifully: And he thought within himself, saying, What shall I do, because I have no room where to bestow my fruits? And he said, This will I do: I will pull down my barns, and build greater; and there will I bestow all my fruits and my goods. And I will say to my soul, Soul, thou hast much goods laid up for many years; take thine ease, eat, drink, and be merry. But God said unto him, Thou fool, this night thy soul shall be required of thee: then whose shall those things be, which thou hast provided? So is he that layeth up treasure for himself, and is not rich toward God. (Lk. 12:15-21)

Which comes first, material things or spiritual things? The shepherds would have found both philosophic materialism and the gross practical materialism Jesus describes in the above parable incongruous with what they had experienced.

Further, as the shepherds looked at the baby Jesus and then walked out of the barn, I think they would have understood the story of Mary and Martha, a story which often confuses readers.

Now it came to pass, as they went, that he [Jesus] entered into a certain village: and a certain woman named Martha received him into her house. And she had a sister called Mary, which also sat at Jesus' feet, and heard his word. But Martha was cumbered about with much serving, and came to him, and said, Lord, dost thou not care that my sister hath left me to serve alone? bid her therefore that she help me. And Jesus answered and said unto her, Martha, Martha, thou art careful and troubled about many things: But one thing is needful: and Mary hath chosen that good part, which shall not be taken away from her. (Lk. 10:38-42)

There is no reason for confusion here. This incident does not deny the necessity of material things. The shepherds would have understood, though, that materialism must never be central, that the "natural" things of life (or whatever terminology one uses for them) must not have first place.

Speaking with Concern and Content

As the shepherds burst out of the stable and began telling people of their experience, certainly they would not have been hard-hearted about whether people believed them or not. Two things can motivate a person to tell the gospel—sheer duty and compassion. The duty is there all right and should not be despised, but it is possible for us to speak as though we were hard-hearted machines. We all need the Lord's forgiveness for this. But hopefully if we were in the shepherds' situation, especially if we had the New Testament informing us that the people were facing an eternal decision for heaven and hell, we would tell the story with genuine concern.

I am not talking about a theological proposition now: Here is my friend, Joe. He sat by the fire with me when the storm came. He stood on the bank and held out his long crook while I waded into the torrent to get a lamb from the rock. My life depended upon his holding on with a hard, calloused hand. We have been companions, standing shoulder to shoulder in difficult times. Good old Joe. In such a situation, I see Joe on the street, and I cry out, "Joe! Joe!" I do not do it just as a duty. I do not have a hard heart but a burning heart.

The burning heart is quite proper. Jesus taught his disciples, "Likewise, I say unto you, there is joy in the presence of the angels of God over one sinner that repenteth" (Lk. 15:10). We could imagine the heavenly hosts viewing this world coolly, observing men and women trooping from birth to death, with some passing from the Kingdom of darkness to the Kingdom of the Son of God's love. But the angels do not have hard hearts; they are glad for everyone that is saved. How wonderful! They never find it dull; they are glad for each one. A new Christian does not become 600,367,001 on the dial. At one time in L'Abri's history, when a person made a profession of faith we played the Hallelujah Chorus. We eventually stopped this because it became mechanical, but when we first did it we did it out of sheer pleasure, thankfulness and joy. All of us should always have this burning heart. May God help us if telling the good news is only a job.

186

Warm-heartedness is, of course, not to be separate from, let alone placed in antithesis to, insistence upon doctrinal content. Evangelism should never be divorced from the reality of who Jesus is. Can we think that these shepherds would have accepted the idea that the great doctrinal truths about this baby did not matter? Imagine them proclaiming the message in the street: All believe! All believe! Then someone comes along and claps one of them on the shoulder: "All right. Never mind about what the angel said. Remove the content and just let us believe." These down-to-the-earth men would never have accepted such a thing. They would have turned around and responded, "Forget the angels and the content they spoke? We can't. They were there."

At the beginning of his Gospel, Luke tells us that the angel came "to a virgin espoused to a man whose name was Joseph, of the house of David; and the virgin's name was Mary" (Lk. 1:27). The angel told her about the child 187 who would come, "He shall be great, and shall be called the Son of the Highest: and the Lord God shall give unto him the throne of his father David: And he shall reign over the house of Jacob for ever; and of his kingdom there shall be no end" (Lk. 1:32-33). Does it matter whether this is true or not? Some may say, "Oh, don't bother with Christ's genealogy. It's of no importance whatsoever." It matters a great deal, however, because Jesus cannot be the Old Testament promised Messiah unless he is from David's line. And even more important is the fact that these verses stress the virgin birth. At the beginning of his life the stress is on the virgin birth.

At the end of his Gospel, in the last chapter of Luke as well as in the first, we have the same great emphasis on doctrine. Here the stress is on his resurrection. In Luke 24 we read,

And as they thus spake, Jesus himself stood in the midst of them, and saith unto them, Peace be unto you. But they were terrified and affrighted, and supposed that they had seen a spirit. And he said unto them, Why are ye troubled? and why do thoughts arise in your hearts? Behold my hands and my feet, that it is I myself: handle me, and see; for a spirit hath not flesh and bones, as ye see me have. And when he had thus spoken, he shewed them his hands and his feet. And while they yet believed not for joy, and wondered, he said unto them, Have ye here any food? And they gave him a piece of a broiled fish, and of an honeycomb. And he took it, and did eat before them. (Lk. 24:36-43)

Doctrine becomes overwhelmingly pressing when one has had an experience such as these men had, and it should be equally pressing to us. We must not let the confusion of modern theological thinking creep in under our door like smog and clog our nose and irritate our eyes so we no longer smell properly or see clearly. The shepherds would not have used the term *doctrinal*, but an old shepherd certainly would have stamped his foot in protest if someone had said, "That's all very nice. I'm so glad you had that experience. But don't talk to me about the reality of what you saw out on the hill." We need some foot-stamping today.

188

Proclaiming, Worshipping, Rejoicing

Doctrinal clarity matters a great deal; but Luke does not allow his Gospel to end merely with a proper emphasis on the necessity of the great doctrinal truths, and our study should not end there either. Before his ascension Jesus told the disciples "that repentance and remission of sins should be preached in his name among all the nations, beginning at Jerusalem" (Lk. 24:47). Orthodox doctrine *must be proclaimed*.

When the shepherds had seen the baby Jesus, "they made known abroad the saying which was told them concerning this child" (Lk. 2:17). Just as the shepherds' proclamation was spontaneous, carrying out Jesus' final instructions should be natural to us. If we really believe the truth of the gospel, we should voluntarily declare it. The spontaneity of telling is part of the Christmas story, whether it is about the babe in the manger or Christ born in my heart.

Yet it is intriguing that the telling is not the final emphasis. The next to the last verse of Luke tells us that the disciples "worshipped him" (Lk. 24:52). The doctrinal reality and the telling of it are never allowed to stand alone; in tremendous balance with it exists worship, personal relationship.

The same thing was true in Bethlehem, in this case with the wise men and the baby Jesus, for "they fell down, and worshipped him" (Mt. 2:11). They did not only bring frankincense and myrrh; they really worshipped. How can we be so foolish and cold-hearted not to understand the necessity of true worship? **189**

But even worship is not the end of the matter: The disciples "returned to Jerusalem with great joy" (Lk. 24: 52). Joy is part of this, too. Certainly the shepherds were glad. The angel had said to them, "Fear not: for, behold, I bring you good tidings of great *joy*, which shall be to all people. For unto you is born this day in the city of David a Saviour, which is Christ the Lord" (Lk. 2: 10-11).

This does not mean a stupid kind of happiness or a sick smile, nor does it mean there are no tears or that things in this world are not as bad as God says they are. This joy is connected with the reality of our knowledge of who Jesus is, our relationship with him and our worship of him.

Imagine you are a shepherd on the hillside, and when the heavenly host appears you are not to be afraid; you are to have joy. It is the same with all the teaching of the

Gospel which flows from the event when the shepherds saw and heard the angels, ran down the hill and looked upon Jesus. Standing at the end of Luke's Gospel, it is reasonable for us to say that, while not despising the doctrine or the telling of it, the central thing is worshipping the Lord—not coldly, but with joy. It is tremendous that the end of the Gospel of Luke could be perfectly at home in the second chapter: "And they worshipped him . . . with great joy."

XII

Jesus
Only

The biblical writers did not make the chapter and verse divisions in our Bibles. These familiar divisions are only convenient index marks which were inserted at a late date, and some of them are poorly placed. Therefore, we must never read the Bible as though we can get any certain unity on the basis of these divisions. Still, because we cannot usually cover an entire book in our study or devotional reading, we tend to stop at the end of chapters, and because we often read a chapter a day, or a certain number of chapters a day, we tend to think of the text in blocks rather than as a flow. Many times this destroys the meaning.

An important illustration of this is found at the end of Matthew 16, where Jesus says, "Verily I say unto you, There be some standing here, which shall not taste of death, till they see the Son of man coming in his kingdom" (Mt. 16:28). This is the end of a chapter, but we should continue reading:

And after six days Jesus taketh Peter, James, and John his brother, and bringeth them up into an high mountain apart, And was transfigured before them: and his face did shine as the sun, and his raiment was white as the light. And, behold, there appeared unto them Moses and Elias talking with him. Then answered Peter, and said unto Jesus, Lord, it is good for us to be here: if thou wilt, let us make here three tabernacles; one for thee, and one for Moses, and one for Elias. While he yet spake, behold, a bright cloud overshadowed them: and behold a voice out of the cloud, which said, This is my beloved Son, in whom I am well pleased; hear ye him. And when the disciples heard it, they fell on their face, and were sore afraid. And Jesus came and touched them, and said, Arise, and be not afraid. And when they had lifted up their eyes, they saw no man, save Jesus only. (Mt. 17:1-8)

194   Matthew 17:1-8 forms a unity with Matthew 16:28. Mark 9:1-7 makes plain that this is the way it should be read. Jesus said that some who were listening to him would see his glory before they died, and his transfiguration followed soon after as the fulfillment of his statement.

The Wonders of the Transfiguration

As we consider the transfiguration itself, many aspects of it should make us marvel. The first wonder of the transfiguration, which has special meaning in the twentieth century, is its space-timeness. Four men walked up a mountain to a certain place, a certain point of geography, just as we would walk up a mountain of Switzerland. The clock was ticking; had the men had watches they could have determined what time it was. Their watches would not have stopped half way up the mountain. Life was still going on in an unbroken way at the bottom of the mountain. There was no break in either time or space. And right in the middle of the space-time world occurred something which men would think of as supernatural—suddenly Moses and Elijah appeared (one long dead, one long ago translated) and Jesus was glorified.

This did not occur merely in someone's thought world. It was not some upper-story situation, where modern theologians would put religious events. Nor was it in an area of a philosophic other. Rather, it was the simplest thing one could imagine, and the most profound: The supernatural occurred in the midst of history. An entire world view is involved in this one concept.

The second wonder of the transfiguration is that Moses and Elijah were present. Moses had died about 1,500 years before Christ, and about 900 years prior to the birth of Jesus Elijah had been taken to heaven without dying; and yet here the two men were, not as wisps of vapor but in recognizable forms. In Moses we see what we will be like between our death and the resurrection of our bodies—if Jesus does not come back before we die. Cartoonists love to draw ghosts coming in through keyholes, but this is not the biblical picture of who we are between our death and our resurrection. A three-way conversation could take place (a propositional, verbalized communication that could be understood by the disciples in normal terms) between Moses, who had died, Elijah, who had been translated, and Christ, who had come up the mountainside.

The third wonder of the transfiguration is that it gives a preview of the resurrection that believers will experience when Jesus returns. As Jesus' transfiguration and resurrection were in the midst of space and time, so too the resurrection of Christians will occur in history and will be historic. The word *historic* does not mean *past*. It means *space-timeness*—that something will occur or has occurred at a certain tick of the clock and at a certain geographic place.

As we reflect further on this third wonder, we can think of Moses as representing the Old Testament dead —all those who for millenia looked forward to the fulfillment of God's promises concerning the coming of Christ as Messiah. Many people, even from the beginning of history through the years before Abraham and the Jews existed, looked forward to the coming of the Messiah with varying degrees of knowledge. The disciples, who were alive at this time but soon would not be, can be thought of as representing the New Testament dead. Peter, James and John have now been dead for almost 2,000 years, and as we think of parents or grandparents who died as Christians, they are represented in these disciples. Thus Old Testament and New Testament believers who have died are represented in this preview of the resurrection.

But who does Elijah represent? 2 Kings 2 tells us he went to heaven without having died. His presence reminds us that a generation of Christians will be alive at the time of the resurrection. Paul wrote about this (and I can never read the passage without Handel's music going through my head):

Behold, I shew you a mystery; We shall not all sleep [that is, we shall not all be dead], but we shall all be changed, In a moment, in the twinkling of an eye, at the last trump: for the trumpet shall sound, and the dead shall be raised incorruptible, and we shall be changed. For this corruptible must put on incorruption, and this mortal must put on immortality. So when this corruptible shall have put on incorruption, and this mortal shall have put on immortality, then shall be brought to pass the saying that is written, Death is swallowed up in victory. (1 Cor. 15:51-54)

Not only are the dead involved in the resurrection but

also those Christians who have not died. On resurrection day, Christ will change these, too, "in the twinkling of an eye."

In 1 Thessalonians Paul gives more details on this subject:

But I would not have you to be ignorant, brethren, concerning them which are asleep, that ye sorrow not, even as others which have no hope. For if we believe that Jesus died and rose again, even so them also which sleep in Jesus will God bring with him. For this we say unto you by the word of the Lord, that we which are alive and remain unto the coming of the Lord shall not precede them which are asleep [those who have died]. For the Lord himself shall descend from heaven with a shout, with the voice of the archangel, and with the trumpet of God: and the dead in Christ shall rise first: Then we which are alive and remain shall be caught up together with them in the clouds, to meet the Lord in the air: and so shall we ever be with the Lord. (1 Thess. 4:13-17)

197

Apparently the Christians in Thessalonica were unsure about what would happen to those already dead. Paul reassured them, "Don't worry. The Christians who have died will be raised first."

Notice that this emphasizes that some Christians will be alive when Jesus returns. Because Paul used the words "then we which are alive," the liberal theologians say that Paul was mistaken. They say he expected to be alive when Jesus returned, but, of course, he has been dead now for centuries. They are wrong; there is no note of that here. Paul is saying that some *Christians* will be alive, using *we* by way of identification. Every Christian should live as though Christ may come back in his own generation. Paul was saying in this phrase, "Some of us Christians will be alive when Jesus comes back again." Each generation of Christians should live, remembering that perhaps they will be the ones to be changed without dying.

The Real Wonder Is Christ

We have spoken about three wonders of the transfiguration: its space-timeness, the presence of Moses and Elijah, and the preview it gives of our future resurrection. The real wonder, however, is Christ himself. The end of the narrative reminds us of its focal point: "And when they had lifted up their eyes, they saw no man, save Jesus only" (Mt. 17:8).

Why Jesus is so important had been revealed to the disciples earlier: "And while he [Jesus] yet spake, behold, a bright cloud overshadowed them: and behold a voice out of the cloud, which said, This is my beloved Son, in whom I am well pleased; hear ye him" (v. 5). The reason the Father said "Hear him" is that Jesus is deity, the eternal second Person of the Trinity. He was, therefore, the center of this whole affair. The center was not Elijah nor Moses, wonderful as their appearance was, nor the disciples; the center was Jesus himself.

It is intriguing that Moses, Elijah and Jesus talked about something. What would you think would be important enough to discuss at such a moment? If we took a poll of people's guesses, I wonder whether any conjecture would be a fit subject for such a titanic moment! However, we need not speculate because Luke tells us they "spake of his decease which he was about to accomplish at Jerusalem" (Lk. 9:31). The only subject worthy of conversation at this moment was Jesus' coming death.

Why was this so? Because Moses, Elijah, the disciples and all the Old and New Testament saints had, and have, a stake in it. If Jesus had not died, everything would have collapsed. Redemption depended on his substitutionary, propitiatory death. If Jesus had not

198

died, if he had turned aside (as Satan tried to make him do so many times), if he had, in Peter's words, actually had pity on himself and not gone onto the cross, everything would have been gone. There would have been no hope for Elijah, translated or not. It would have meant the end of Moses, the disciples and everyone else, because the redemption of everything depended on the single focal point of Jesus' death. John the Baptist, the last Old Testament prophet, had proclaimed as he introduced Jesus to the Jews, "Behold the Lamb of God, which taketh away the sin of the world" (John 1:29), and no other conversation was big enough for the Mount of Transfiguration. Jesus' resurrection is certainly important. So too are his ascension and his teachings. But the welfare of every believer and the entire creation depends upon his death.

Yes, the real wonder is Christ, the eternal Son of God who came to earth to die, who was glorified on the Mount of Transfiguration: And he "was transfigured before them: and his face did shine as the sun, and his raiment was white as the light" (v. 2). We can think of this as the prefiguration of his coming resurrection body.

After his resurrection he had a body that could still be touched and could still eat, but it was changed so that he could move back and forth from the seen to the unseen world, as he did many times in the forty days after his resurrection. He would appear—on the road to Emmaus or in a room and then no longer be seen. Then Jesus' glorification continued in the ascension, when, as an official act, as the conclusion of his earthly ministry, Christ with his resurrected body left the earth.

What is Jesus like now? At least three times since Jesus ascended men have seen him. I am not saying that other men may not have seen him since the ascension, but the Bible records only three instances. The first was

Stephen when he was being stoned. The second was Paul on the road to Damascus:

> And Saul, yet breathing out threatenings and slaughter against the disciples of the Lord, went unto the high priest, And desired of him letters to Damascus to the synagogues, that if he found any of this way, whether they were men or women, he might bring them bound unto Jerusalem. And as he journeyed, he came near Damascus: and suddenly there shined round about him a light from heaven: And he fell to the earth, and heard a voice saying unto him, Saul, Saul, why persecutest thou me? And he said, Who art thou, Lord? And the Lord said, I am Jesus whom thou persecutest. (Acts 9:1-5)

Here Christ, as he was prefigured in the transfiguration, appeared to Saul as glorified. This meeting with Saul was personal. Jesus was not just a concept, an idea or an abstraction; he was a person who spoke to Saul in the Hebrew language. And he called Saul by his name. The glorified Christ spoke in propositional, verbalized communication in normal literary categories.

200

The other man who saw Jesus after the ascension is John, who was at the time of the appearance an old man and a prisoner on the isle of Patmos, the Roman equivalent of a concentration camp. On the Lord's day, Sunday, the first day of the week, his attention was arrested by a voice behind him. He turned around and saw the glorified Christ. As you read what he saw, notice carefully the words *like* and *as*. These are important because the text is not saying, for example, that Jesus' hair is wool; John is using what we can understand to describe Christ in his glory as he is now:

> His head and his hair were white like wool, as white as snow; and his eyes were as a flame of fire; And his feet like unto fine brass, as if they burned in a furnace; and his voice as the sound of many waters. And he

had in his right hand seven stars: and out of his mouth went a sharp twoedged sword: and his countenance was as the sun shineth in his strength. And when I saw him, I fell at his feet as dead. And he laid his right hand upon me, saying unto me, Fear not; I am the first and the last: I am the living one that became dead; and, behold, I am alive for evermore, Amen; and have the keys of death and of hades. (Rev. 1:14-18)

As with Paul on the Damascus road, notice the strong personal element here. Jesus laid his right hand upon John and in effect said: "Don't be afraid. I, though glorified, am the same Jesus upon whose breast you rested before I died."

This was Jesus as John saw him there on the island of Patmos—Jesus glorified. When he walked with the disciples day after day, in many ways he was like any man striding along through the dust of Palestine. But on the Mount of Transfiguration, in the resurrection and then in the three post-ascension appearances, men saw him as we shall when we see him. In the transfiguration he was glorified, prefiguring what he is like now and what he will be like when we see him in the future face to face.

"They Saw No Man, Save Jesus Only"

Having seen that Jesus is the real wonder and center of the transfiguration account, let us focus on the conclusion of the narrative: When the disciples finally lifted up their eyes, "they saw no man, save Jesus only" (Mt. 17:8). This is not to be confused with looking at Jesus in contrast to, or instead of, the Father and the Holy Spirit —a mistake which I am convinced Christians sometimes make. We are not being told, "Look at Jesus. Don't look at the Father or the Holy Spirit." It is a doctrinal and psychological mistake to think that Jesus eclipses the rest of the Trinity. The passage is rather saying, "Don't look at other men. Look at Jesus." When we are looking at him (and we could say the same about the rest of the Trinity), that vision eclipses all others. In this sense, then, our minds are to be on Jesus only.

I would suggest several ways in which we are to remember that it is Jesus only. The first is to remember that Christ is at the center of all time.

Along with classical Buddhists and Hindus, who teach that everything is returning to the pantheistic whole, modern man believes history is going nowhere. To the twentieth-century thinker, history is absurd, or at most an endless series of cycles going nowhere, and nothing really matters. But the scriptural view is entirely different. History is not static; this Jesus who was glorified on the Mount of Transfiguration has existed forever. He was before the creation of the space-time continuum, and "all things were made by him" (John 1:3).

202 The Greek verb in this phrase is in the aorist tense, which means that something new occurred; at creation something that did not exist before came into existence once and for all. This was not just a creation from eternity or a timeless coming-forthness, a becomingness, but an event that happened at one point rather than another.

After the creation of space-time history, history has flowed on, and Jesus stands at the center of it. As soon as the Fall took place, God directed man's mind to the coming of Jesus: We are told that immediately after man's revolt against God the promise came that the seed of the woman would bruise the serpent's head (Gen. 3:15). This immediately gave all history a perspective-point. History is absurd to the modern man because he has no perspective-point. It is as though there were no perspective in a drawing; nothing would seem to hang together. But God immediately gave a perspective in history—the end of the railroad tracks, as it were, bringing the lines together from all places and times. And that perspective-point, as soon as man fell, was the future coming of the woman's seed.

Now that Jesus has come, we, of course, look back to that event. God, in his providence, constantly does things that men cannot eliminate—no matter how much they want to get rid of God. One of these is the curious historic "accident" that arranges all the calendars of the world around Christ. The Jews can put another date on the cornerstones of their synagogues, but in their day-to-day existence they must date their life by the coming of Christ. Nobody has been able to change this. Even the communist world has an A.D. and a B.C. I am sure that in the future the Antichrist, or somebody, will try to work out a new dating system to get rid of Christ in time, but now whenever you write a date, you are saying, "This man is the center of history." If you are not a Christian when you stand before God in judgment, **203** one of the many things God will have to talk with you about will be all the dates you have written on your letters.

Jesus is not only central to history as we look backward, but also as we look forward to his return. For example, when Paul writes that the Lord's Supper looks back to the death of Jesus, he teaches that it also looks forward: "For as often as ye eat this bread, and drink this cup, ye do shew the Lord's death till he come" (1 Cor. 11:26). So history has a perspective-point, the Lord Jesus Christ, and a flow—the promise given at the Fall, the death of Christ, his second coming. History, therefore, has meaning. So as we concentrate on Jesus only, we can remember that he is at the center of all time.

Jesus is the center to us as individuals as well. The call to a non-Christian is to make Jesus the center of his life. The call to Christians is to remember that he is the center. We think of his finished work on the cross, for if

Jesus' death is not the center of our hope of being accepted by God, we are lost. It is as simple as that. If we bring in humanistic things and in any way make them the center, our hope is destroyed. But Jesus is not to be the center only at conversion. He is to be central in our living as well, in both comprehension and practice. God the Father told the disciples, "Hear him."

In Reformation theology, the offices of Christ are designated as prophet, priest and king. He is described as the great prophet because he gave us additional knowledge about God. He is different from the other prophets in that he spoke with authority from himself. He revealed the Godhead bodily. It amazed the people who heard him that he did not speak like John the Baptist, for example, who had spoken with the authority of someone else. Today Jesus the living word, together with Scripture the written word, still teaches us about God. Without the knowledge we have from the living word (Jesus) and the written word (the Bible), we know nothing properly; we do not know things in their ultimate relationships.

But Christian faith is not only a matter of knowledge. Christ must be the center of a Christian's life. True spirituality is not our producing something in the external world but Christ producing his fruit through us. This he does through the indwelling of the Holy Spirit as we put ourselves in his hands.

We should reflect the mentality of John the Baptist: "He must increase, but I must decrease" (John 3:30). Our conscious practice should be that Jesus Christ is the only Person who is indispensable. By this, I mean that other people can take our place. God does use individuals. You and I are not two interchangeable building blocks. The individual person has importance to God. But we are dispensable in the sense that as we come to the end of our work for God in this life, because of either

204

death or failure, there will be someone to carry on, because Jesus himself is the center of the work.

This was the mentality of Paul; he regarded himself as a slave of Jesus Christ. When Christians in Corinth argued "I was saved by Apollos" versus "I was saved by Paul," Paul responded, "Aren't you stupid! What an argument!" He said, "Who then is Paul, and who is Apollos, but ministers by whom ye believed, even as the Lord gave to every man? I have planted, Apollos watered; but God gave the increase. So then neither is he that planteth any thing, neither he that watereth; but God that giveth the increase" (1 Cor. 3:5-7). Paul had one ministry, Apollos another; their personalities did not disappear, but Jesus gave the ministry. It is important how we labor, yet our basic mentality should be this: I am by choice a bond servant, and it is my master who is central, not me. When this is not our mentality we have lost our way.

205

Through the centuries when one servant of God has laid down the burden of God's work, another has picked it up. The one who has picked it up has had a different personality than his predecessor, but God's work has continued.

We could give many examples. Cain killed Abel, but God's work did not end because Seth was born to carry on the line. Abraham was followed by Isaac who was followed by Jacob. When Jacob died, Joseph was there to carry on. Joseph died, and in due time came Moses. Joshua followed him. These men had their own personalities; all were meaningful. No one was a machine or puppet. Nevertheless, they were not at the center of history's stage.

The judges of Israel came one after another, some failing, all dying, but God's work continued. We say with tears that Eli failed, but the little boy Samuel was already on the scene. King Saul failed dismally; David carried on. Later in the northern kingdom Elijah's ministry of confronting the great was succeeded by Elisha's quieter one. In the southern kingdom Isaiah died but in due time Jeremiah was there to continue.

The prophets Ezekiel and Daniel came next. When Daniel was ready to lay down his burden in death, God had Zerubbabel ready. Later Ezra came, then Nehemiah. In the New Testament, Paul laid down the burden, and Timothy and a host of elders followed, and the church flows on.

Each one of these men was fitted to his moment of history; each one carried on in a different way; each of their personalities was valid. None of them, however, was at the center; and to the extent that any of them got taken up with his own importance, he missed his real place. None stood at the center, but at the center was a Person greater than any man: a Person who gave meaning to each man's non-centeredness. Similarly, Christ must be the center of the perspective of every Christian —not only in his doctrine but in his day-by-day outlook.

Rivals to Jesus

Having stressed that Jesus must be in the center of our lives, I want to mention four other things that we must be careful not to put there. The first is any totalitarian state or totalitarian church. If I have the perspective the disciples had on the Mount of Transfiguration—"this is my beloved Son . . . hear ye him"—there is no place for a totalitarian anything! Neither a church which puts itself between the individual and God nor a state which demands primary allegiance has such a right. There is a legitimate place for both the state and church, but not at the center. The center must be a Person.

Totalitarian, authoritative states are not far from us. They breathe down our necks at every turn, not only communist countries but also modern elites in the West.

206

Not only the elite of the Marcuse New Left but the John Galbraith establishment elite puts itself in the center, too. In each case, an authoritative society offers itself as the integration point. The Christian must always say, "I want the state and society to have its proper place. But if it tries to come into the center of my life, *I am against it* because Jesus only is there."

This danger is more subtle in a religious setting, and especially in an evangelical setting, when manifested as a totalitarian, authoritative, human leadership. Because this too is often pressing upon us, we should be careful at every turn. There is to be human leadership in the church, under the leadership of the Holy Spirit, but it is wrong for men, even good men, to take the center for themselves. Paul's mentality, as we have seen, was not this. Neither was John the Baptist's. Only the Triune God may be central. The danger does not have to come from a Hitler or Stalin. It can come from a Christian 207 who gets so caught up in the mechanics of leadership that, unwittingly or not, he puts himself where only God should be.

If we lived in a totalitarian state, we would be well aware of it. And even totalitarian, authoritative leadership in a church probably makes us feel uncomfortable, like a coat that is too tight. More difficult to detect, however, is making a phase of Christian work central instead of Christ and the Trinity. When Christian work becomes the integration point, it too is wrong.

It is curious that we can do things in Christ's name while pushing him off the stage. I have seen this most plainly when a church has become caught up in a building project and has moved heaven and earth to complete it. One does need a roof over his head, but this is only a small portion of the church's ministry. The building is only an instrument.

Fighting for evangelism and the salvation of souls

should not become primary either, yet how often this happens! Other people, quite rightly see the church of our generation threatened by apostasy, but then have made the purity of the visible church the center of their life. In all of these Jesus may remain as a topic of conversation but his real centrality be forgotten. In the name of Christ, Christ is dethroned. When this happens, even what is right becomes wrong.

More subtle still is making certain doctrines central. For instance we can reason: I am a Presbyterian so I will emphasize above all the doctrine of predestination. The sovereignty of God is to be taught, but some of my friends have stressed it so much that the doctrine, not God, has become the center of their ministry. This can be done with other doctrines. Surely you have known people who have so emphasized the type of baptism a person should have that it has become the center of conversation, the center of the battle, really, the center of perspective. As soon as we do this with any doctrine, it is like a flat tire that makes the whole car bump.

In reality there is only one center, not only as a doctrine but in practice—Christ and the Trinity. What does the God who is there have to say about himself? As soon as we answer this question and live on the basis of it, everything fits into place, like a nicely ordered closet or a beautiful piece of music by Bach, in which every voice has its place.

God at the Center

Finally, let me stress that I myself must not be in the center. When I am, my perspective gets completely distorted. In Matthew 16 there is another statement that flows into the seventeenth chapter: "Then said Jesus unto his disciples, if any man will come after me, let him deny himself, and take up his cross, and follow me" (Mt. 16:24). It is superficial to think this only means that a

Christian should be willing to suffer. It means he should not put himself at the center of reality; he is not in theory or practice to be his own integration point. A person may be willing to be a martyr and to do God's work with great sacrifice and yet not really be denying himself in this sense. Denying one's self means simply that, in thought and practice, we resist our own personal humanism. We cannot stand at the center of the universe, and when we try to we must tell the Lord we are sorry.

A Christian's proper denial is not like a pantheist's. In the East you deny your personality: You say it is not important and you strive for nirvana, in which your personality will finally be lost. But the Bible teaches you have a right to your personality because you are made in the image of God. You have a right to fulfillment because God is so interested in your total person that he is going to raise your body from the dead. Still, you cannot be at the center of things, because you are only a creature. **209** You are dependent. Only God is independent.

As a Christian, I must deny myself in this deep and profound sense, and I cannot do it once for all. I must have a constant, moment-by-moment understanding that God is at the center. I must put second all other things that God has made, especially the centrality of *Me*. I must have the perspective of the disciples as they looked up and "saw no man, save Jesus only."

The
Water
of
Life

When Jesus attended the Feast of the Tabernacles in his final year, the time of his popularity was past. Once great crowds had followed him everywhere. The feeding of the five thousand had been the high point of this kind of popularity. After that, however, as he stressed more and more who he was and what his work really was, the crowds dwindled. He went through a period of retirement in Galilee just prior to the Feast, and then at this time Peter uttered his words of confession. The context in which this is recorded emphasizes that many had turned away: "From that time many of his disciples went back, and walked no more with him. Then said Jesus unto the twelve, Will ye also go away? Then Simon Peter answered him, Lord, to whom shall we go? thou hast the words of eternal life. And we believe and are sure that thou art that Christ, the Son of the living God" (John 6:66-69). Peter stands in sharp contrast to those disciples who left Jesus and to the crowds who turned away, for he said, "We believe and know [*know* is better than *are sure* for this Greek verb] that you are the Christ."

As the Feast of the Tabernacles approached,
Jesus walked in Galilee, for he would not walk in Jewry [Judea], because the Jews sought to kill him. Now the Jews' feast of tabernacles was at hand. His brethren therefore said to him, Depart hence, and go into Judea, that thy disciples also may see the works that thou doest. For there is no man that doeth anything in secret, and he himself seeketh to be known openly. If thou do these things, shew thyself to the world. For neither did his brethren believe in him. (John 7:1-5)

Many who become Christians have difficulty with their unbelieving families. They can be comforted by realizing that Jesus himself experienced the pain of such a situation. Those children born to Mary and Joseph did not believe on him until after his resurrection; his own brothers gibed at him harshly.

To understand what came next, we must visualize Jerusalem during the Feast of the Tabernacles. It is estimated that well over a million people from all over the known world, both Jews and proselytes, poured into it. People milled about like ants on an ant hill. The city was full of religious fervor. The crowd was a great mixture, including God-fearers and formalists, Sadducees (the rationalists) and Pharisees (the orthodox who had allowed their orthodoxy to become formalized and dead). True believers would have been in it—people who waited for the Lord's redemption through the Messiah, like Simeon and Anna. Some were there merely to sell trinkets. Prostitutes undoubtedly walked up and down the streets. The city reflected both the glory of the Old Testament prophecies and the low level of Jewish religious life at that time.

Jesus walked into this scene and associated the Feast

of the Tabernacles with himself. (In Luke 22:19 he did the same with the Passover, so when we apply these feasts to Jesus we do so on his authority.) And during the festival he received challenge after challenge to his ever-clear teaching about who he is.

The Great Day of the Feast

The Feast of the Tabernacles was so named because God had commanded the Jews to live in tabernacles during this period each year to remind them that they had had to live in temporary abodes as they moved through the wilderness after the exodus. Through the centuries since then, and still today, the Jews have enacted this reminder. During the wanderings, God twice provided water from a rock, so the feast reenacted this, too. In fact the remembrance of this had developed as a technical part of the festival and had tremendous importance. On the final day, "the great day of the feast," 213 came the great rite of pouring out water in the presence of the people to represent God's provision in the desert. Non-biblical sources reveal that the force of the fervor that built up as people waited for this outpouring, the sheer religiosity of the situation, was almost unbearable. As the water was poured out, the Feast came to its climax.

It was just at this point in the festival that Jesus stood up (he must have stood in one of the raised places in the temple area so he could be seen) and gave what was probably the boldest invitation of his entire ministry: "If any man thirst, let him come unto me, and drink. He that believeth on me, as the Scripture hath said, out of his belly shall flow rivers of living water" (John 7:37-38). He said this, we note again, in the context of the remembrance in every Jew's mind that God had twice given rivers of water from a smitten rock.

He clearly appealed here to the innermost cravings of

men and women. The word *thirst* connotes severe long-ing. We immediately think of idioms like "a thirst for knowledge" and "a thirst for life." In the former idiom, *thirst* communicates a craving for knowledge that will not tolerate being unsatisfied and will do whatever is necessary to have the knowledge. The latter reminds us of tremendous exploits like those so rich in the memory of the Swiss, of men falling into huge ice crevasses and even with broken hips digging themselves out with an ice axe, taking hundreds of steps while suffering horri-ble pain simply to hang onto physical life.

Those who have experienced a shortage of water al-ways link water most closely with the desire for life. An American Indian from the Western desert was invited to New York many years ago. When he had seen every-thing, he was asked, "What impressed you most?" He walked to a water tap, turned it on and replied, "Water whenever you want it." Such a reaction is typical of peo-ple who have known thirst.

We can see this in Spanish architecture. When the Saracens came into Spain with its abundance of water, they never forgot the lack they had known in North Afri-ca. They made the magnificent fountains of Seville, which spring up on every side as you walk along the streets and through the palace grounds. The alabaster fountains, which with little water produce the sound of much water, are marvels of Saracen craftsmanship.

And so it was in Palestine. The connection of water with life was deeply imbedded in the collective con-sciousness of the Jewish race. All Jews remembered the need for water. The patriarchs Abraham, Isaac and Jacob had been forced to move their flocks to find it. Hezekiah had had to come up with a tremendous engineering feat, a tunnel, to provide water in order to withstand a siege of Jerusalem. Water always brought to the Jewish mind their own struggle for survival.

David in his psalms uses the image of thirst to represent a total, rather than half-hearted, following after something. In Psalm 42 he cries out, "As the hart panteth after the water brooks, so panteth my soul after thee, O God. My soul thirsteth for God, for the living God" (Ps. 42:1-2). In Psalm 63 he declares, "O God, thou art my God; early will I seek thee: my soul thirsteth for thee, my flesh longeth for thee in a dry and thirsty land, where no water is" (Ps. 63:1). And, of course, we cannot forget Psalm 23, two verses of which involve thirsting and understanding what it means to have water in abundance: "He maketh me to lie down in green pastures: he leadeth me beside the still waters.... My cup runneth over" (vv. 2, 5). The Lord provides ample waters fit for his sheep to drink.

The sources of this imagery, which the Jews had as part of their consciousness and understood deep inside themselves, were both the quest for physical life and the yearning after God. So when Jesus used the word *thirst* it had a double significance, coming from their culture and from Scripture: It was a strong word literally meaning *really-reaching-out-for* and metaphorically suggesting spiritual longing.

A Meaning for Life

Jesus, then, was not just using *water* in its physical sense. What he was talking about has reference to both present life and life after death. Orthodox Christians have always stressed the life after death, and quite properly. This is emphasized much in Scripture. Perhaps we have not stressed sufficiently, however, the meaning for life *now*, which the aspirations of our own century remind us is also in Scripture. In the Bible these two are never set against each other but are carried together.

Jesus reminded his hearers of this most intense physical longing and related it to the most basic need beyond that for physical life—the necessity for a present meaning to life as we live it. In this sense, the word *existential* is a good one: Men want an *existential* meaning for life— a meaning for life at this tick of the clock, at this point in space and time. Then they want a horizontal projection of it into the afterlife.

These are the real aspirations of men. We find them expressed in prehistoric caves and in modern studies in comparative religion. As we examine the cultures of the world, we find individual atheists but no really atheistic society. Atheism is the official position of the Soviet Union, but the mass of people have yet to be seen living out its implications. There remains in men of all cultures a universal longing for both—meaning to life now and life after death.

Walk through the metaphysical strata of men's philosophies and you find exactly the same thing. It is a special annoyance of mine that men try to separate philosophy and religion. This is a false separation, because both ultimately seek the meaning of life.

216

As we walk with men from the past and the present, with simple men and complicated men, with men of the East or the West, it makes no difference—wherever men are, they search for a meaning to life. St. Augustine framed this thinking as he addressed God in the well-known words, "Thou hast created us for thyself, O God, and we cannot rest until we find our rest in thee." Augustine knew the Greek thinking and the metaphysical and religious thinking of his own day, but he spoke from the Judeo-Christian perspective and let in light on man's search for purpose. He related meaning to a personal God who is the Creator and who is there. At the Feast of the Tabernacles Jesus spoke in this framework.

Man's thirsting can only be satisfied within a framework that answers two questions: What is the meaning of man, and why is he in the dilemma he is in? The Scripture had already outlined for the Jews the reason for man's dilemma, namely, man's Fall, his rebellion against God. It is not because there is no one to speak with that men are lonely, but because they are cut off from the one who can fulfill their loneliness. If man is a being kicked up by chance without any intrinsic meaning for his life, then Jesus' words would not have been blasphemous, for there would be no one to blaspheme; they would simply have been ridiculous—only one more banner to follow in a hopeless crusade. But Jesus spoke in a definite framework, affirming that man is lost but not intrinsically lost, because he was not made to be lost.

Man is guilty, but there is a solution. Jesus stood up on the great day of the Feast and, in a solid framework which he shared with the other Jews, offered himself to fill the real needs of men: "If any man thirst, let him come unto me and drink." "I am the answer," Jesus was saying. "I am the water of life." This must have caused upheaval in that intense setting.

Jesus' Exclusive Message
It is essential to understand that Jesus' message was completely exclusive. He offered himself not as *a solution* to life but as *the one* who can fulfill man's innermost longings. He was saying, "I am *the* water of life." This, of course, parallels many other times when he hammered home the definite articles with great clarity, saying, for example, "I am *the* way, *the* truth and *the* life."

Jesus had given promises like the one at the Feast before, but never in an official capacity. In almost exactly the same words, he had offered this satisfaction to the woman at the well: "If thou knewest the gift of God, and who it is that sayest to thee, Give me to drink; thou wouldest have asked of him, and he would have given thee living water. . . . Whosoever drinketh of the water that I shall give him shall never thirst; but the water that I shall give him shall be in him a well of water springing up into everlasting life" (John 4:10, 14). Though the woman was a Samaritan, she understood that according to the Old Testament Scriptures a personal Messiah was to come in history; therefore she responded, "I know that Messias cometh, which is called Christ: when he is come, he will tell us all things" (John 4:25). Then Jesus made a clear declaration of his person: "I that speak unto thee am he" (John 4:26). Jesus said exactly the same thing as at the Feast. The difference is that the one was a personal saying to one person, the other an official declaration.

Later he made this promise to a group of people rather than to an individual, but again it was not an official statement to the nation: "I am the bread of life: he that cometh to me shall never hunger; and he that believeth on me shall never thirst" (John 6:35). Further on he said to them,

> Verily, verily, I say unto you, Except ye eat the flesh of the Son of man, and drink his blood, ye have no life in you. Whoso eateth my flesh, and drinketh my blood, hath eternal life; and I will raise him up at the last day. For my flesh is meat indeed, and my blood is drink indeed. He that eateth my flesh, and drinketh my blood, dwelleth in me and I in him. (John 6:53-56)

So at least twice before the Feast of the Tabernacles, Jesus had declared himself to be the water of life, the one who can quench the real thirst of men.

Jesus' statement at the Feast was different in one important respect: It was a regal proclamation to the whole nation gathered at the religious center of the world. If Athens is the metropolis of learning, Jerusalem is the metropolis of true religion. It is Zion, the city of God. It is Jesus' city, and one day he will rule there. As the people of his nation crowded into this chosen scene, Jesus held himself aloft as fulfilling the tremendous Old Testament prophecies. We could think, for example, of a statement by Isaiah, "Ho, every one that thirsteth, come ye to the waters, and he that hath no money; come ye, buy, and eat; yea, come, buy wine and milk without money and without price" (Is. 55:1).

So on the great day of the feast that commemorated the wilderness wanderings, with the Jewish nation assembled to watch the water being poured out to remind them of miraculous water given twice from a rock, Jesus stood and, in the face of rising opposition to his claim, made one of the strongest statements of his entire ministry: "I am the true water. Come unto me and drink."

The Meaning of Drinking

What did Jesus mean when he spoke of drinking? Is this simply an incomprehensible metaphor? Not at all, for he himself made the meaning clear. He immediately followed the statement "If any man thirst, let him come unto me, and drink" with the phrase "He that believeth on me." And John's inspired editorial comment leaves no doubt that Jesus was talking about faith: "But this spake he of the Spirit, which they that believe on him should receive" (John 7:39). He was not speaking of a sacramental drinking, in the sense of a cup to be quaffed, but of something much more profound—believing on him.

In his less formal statements about being the water of life, he also made plain who he is. Jesus always connected teaching about his person, who he is, with teaching about his work and his ability to fill men's needs. In the dialogue recorded in John 6, five times he referred to himself as the one who came down from heaven (vv. 33, 38, 41, 42 and 51). And verse 62 makes it impossible for anyone to maintain, "Oh, he's only saying he's an especially heavenly man," for it puts this description in the special framework in which he meant it: "What and if ye shall see the Son of man ascend up where he was before?" He is not saying he is a bit more heavenly than other men, but he is making a claim about his own nature, his own person—that he really came from heaven, that he is the second Person of the Trinity, that he is the Son of God. The Jews understood his message well enough to shout, "Blasphemy!"

More than that, some of these listeners would see him going to heaven in a special sense on the day of his ascension. When modern men try to cut out his official leavetaking, they attack Jesus' own teaching of who he is.

In this conversation in John 6 he also emphasized what it means to eat and drink him. When the people asked, "What shall we do, that we might work the works of God? Jesus answered and said unto them, This is the work of God, that ye believe on him whom he hath sent" (John 6:28-29). There is only one way for a fallen man to work the work of God, and that is to believe on him whom the Father has sent. Jesus made plain that the eating and drinking is not a sacramental eating and drinking at a communion service: "I am the bread of life: he that cometh to me shall never hunger; and he that believeth on me shall never thirst" (John 6:35). It is not by eating and drinking the Lord's Supper that we are saved. It is *believing on Christ* that matters.

A Personal Decision

Each person who heard Jesus' invitation on the great day of the Feast was faced with a decision—would he believe or not? And every person who hears the invitation of Jesus Christ in the second half of the twentieth century is faced with the same decision. Whether you hear it through the preached Word of God or through reading the Scriptures (Jesus himself related his invitation to the

Scripture: "He that believeth on me, as the scripture hath said..."), this invitation gives you only two choices: to accept or reject him, to believe on him or cry with the crowd, "Not Christ but Barabbas. Crucify him!" There is no neutrality, no alternative, no third choice. They could not say, "He is a nice man." On the basis of Jesus' claim, either the Jews had to believe on him or they had to cry out against him.

A Spiritual Torrent

When we accept Christ as our Savior, do we receive only a streamlet of blessing? Is it only like the few drops which drip out of a pipe after the water is turned off? As D. L. Moody once remarked about this verse, "No, a thousand times no." Jesus promised, "He that believeth on me, as the scripture hath said, out of his belly [his innermost parts] shall flow *rivers* of living water." A river, a torrent, a Niagara—this is what flows.   **221**

From whence does the river come? From someplace to which I must make a pilgrimage? Must I go to some special place, for example, Huemoz? Happily, no. When a man believes, it is out of himself that the rivers of living water flow. John gives the explanation in an inspired form so we do not need to guess at Jesus' meaning: "But this spake he of the Spirit, which they that believe on him should receive: for the Holy Spirit was not yet given; because that Jesus was not yet glorified" (John 7:39).

It is made plain that Jesus must be struck *once* before the rivers can be given. In the wilderness, when the water was given, the rock had to be struck once, but it was wrong to strike it twice (Ex. 17 and Num. 20). This was because when the rock was struck once that finished the picture of the work of Jesus Christ. In order for the work of salvation to be accomplished and the Holy Spirit to be given, Jesus had to be struck once, but he will not be struck twice. Jesus appeared at the right time and died once for all on Calvary's cross in space and time. When he was done, he said, "The work is finished." Later the same testimony was given by Peter and by the writer of Hebrews: Jesus' death was once for all.

Jesus was hung on the cross, he was pierced, he died. Though he cried out from Calvary, "My God, my God, why hast thou forsaken me?" this was not his last word. Rather, he said "It is finished" and turned to the Father, "Father, into thy hands I commend my spirit." The work is done, and since Pentecost every person who believes on Jesus as his Savior has the Holy Spirit, the Spirit of Christ, the Spirit of truth—all these are words for the same Person—living within him. The Holy Spirit, not some inner strength or psychological integratedness, is the source of the overflowing rivers of living water. There are to be living waters, a watered garden in the time of drought. The Holy Spirit lives within!

Not only are these rivers to be copious, they are also to be diffused; the "rivers of living water" are to *flow*, flow out to others. The Holy Spirit is not to be kept selfishly within myself, like a treasure clutched in a small child's fist. The waters are not to be dammed up until they become a stagnant pool. They are to be a flowing, flowing, flowing river.

Nor are the rivers to be contaminated before they flow forth to others. As the rivers flow from us, if we are children of God through faith in Jesus Christ, they are not to be contaminated with either impure doctrine or an impure life, both of which bring contamination. There was a day when the Delaware River (I was raised in Philadelphia so the Delaware River means something special to me) was rich in fish. You cannot find a fish there now no matter how hard you try. The contamination in the upper Delaware has killed them all.

I could take you to a stream near Huemoz where

women used to go to wash their clothes. They could take pails and carry them home full of clear water. This stream was once teeming with life. Now it is contaminated, defiled by the waste of Villars and Chesieres. I hate to cross it, and I try to find ways around it so I do not have to be reminded that this creation was once beautiful. It still flows, but the life is gone.

Dr. Tom Lambie, one of the great missionaries to Africa, concluded that the height of a civilization can be measured by the amount of contamination in its drinking water. Think of the modern pollution of our water supplies! I would say to you in the name of Jesus Christ that the degree of the infidelity of an individual Christian or a Christian group to the Word of God in doctrine and life is shown by the amount of contamination in the water which flows forth.

So let us ask ourselves as Christians how we contaminate the waters that flow from us. The Bible does not promise perfection in this life. But, by God's grace, let us stop quenching the Spirit who lives within us so that our lives may show forth the Spirit's fruit. How terrible it is to be Bible-believing Christians, to fight for orthodoxy, to fight for the evangelical position, and then to contaminate the water we hold out to others. How terrible—for these waters have been given to us without cost, brimming over, pure, directly from the fountainhead!

Are you still thirsting? Christ gives the invitation not only to others but to you. He is the fountainhead. He has died and is risen. He offers the only way to eternal life, asking only that you admit your needs, raise the empty hands of faith and accept his gift. What is eternal life? It is meaning in life now as well as living one's life forever. Drink deep. Jesus offers a brimming cup.

The Book of Revelation: Future Yet a Unity with the Present

The book of Revelation is, of course, the last book of the Bible. It completes the unity of the Old and New Testaments, and the total gives us what we need until the second coming of Christ. Beginning with chapter 4 the book of Revelation speaks primarily of future historic events. It gives us propositional truth concerning things of the future. Like all the Bible it is a propositional communication from the Infinite Personal God to finite personal man, made in God's image. It tells us things which will happen in future space and time. Because the Infinite God has not put chance back of himself when he created a significant history, he can tell us of future events as well as past events. History is going some place; it is not a series of endless cycles. History as we now know it had an absolute starting place at the creation, and it flows on. This era will end with the future space-time coming of Christ and his reign upon the earth. Yet, while the whole of Scripture, including the book of Revelation, stresses the reality, the historicity of future events, by no means does it totally separate the future from the past and present. The past, present and future are intimately connected.

An excellent illustration is found in a prophecy of Joel: And it shall come to pass afterward, that I will pour out my spirit upon all flesh; and your sons and your daughters shall prophesy, your old men shall dream dreams, your young men shall see visions: And also upon the servants and upon the handmaids in those days will I pour out my spirit. And I will shew wonders in the heavens and in the earth, blood, and fire, and pillars of smoke. The sun shall be turned into darkness, and the moon into blood, before the great and the terrible day of the LORD come. And it shall come to pass, that whosoever shall call on the name of the LORD shall be delivered: for in mount Zion and in **226** Jerusalem shall be deliverance, as the LORD hath said, and in the remnant whom the LORD shall call. (Joel 2:28-32)

God told Joel that someday the Holy Spirit would work in a new way in people's hearts. Centuries later, Pentecost fulfilled a large portion of the prophecy. The Holy Spirit began to work with the people of God in a new way, a way unlike his Old Testament working, for, from Pentecost to today, he has immediately indwelt each person who accepts Christ as Savior.

Yet not all of Joel's prophecy was fulfilled at Pentecost. God's covenant with Abraham had had two portions, one spiritual, the other natural or national. We Christians stand in the stream of the spiritual portion, but the natural portion is not yet in its totality fulfilled. Since God does not lie, he will fulfill his promise to the Jews as Jews, and those Jews who are alive at the second coming of the Lord Jesus Christ will be saved and the Holy Spirit will then indwell them as he came to the Christians at

Pentecost. Paul, writing on this side of the open tomb, prophesied, "And so all Israel shall be saved: as it is written, There shall come out of Sion the Deliverer, and shall turn away ungodliness from Jacob . . . . For the gifts and calling of God are not repented of" (Rom. 11:26-29).

Thus Joel's prophecy involves both our present and Israel's future. The Jews in the future will be saved on the same basis that we Christians (Jews or Gentiles) are saved in the present, by the finished work of the Old Testament-prophesied Messiah, the Lamb of God, and they will be saved to the same end.

This is not a matter of double fulfillment, where the prophecy was once fulfilled at every point and will be completely fulfilled again. Rather, it is a diversity within a total unity. So as we study the book of Revelation, we do not have to make a choice between the future and a present meaning for us now. There is a flow of history, a diversity of detail in the midst of a continuing unity. From the fourth chapter on, the book of Revelation speaks of a future time, but this is not unconnected to the historical present.

This relationship parallels the unity and yet diversity between the Old and New Testament eras. Men in both eras are saved by the finished work of Christ. Old Testament worship was couched in terms of prophecy about the coming Messiah. Worshippers on this side of the cross know the prophecy has been fulfilled. Christians do not worship by bringing a lamb to an altar. Likewise, there will be a future era, with which the past and the present will share important things in common.

The First Great Unity: The Existence and Character of God
As we read Revelation 4, we soon discover one of the great truths that unify the past, present and future: "And the four beasts had each of them six wings about him; and they were full of eyes within: and they rest

not day and night, saying, Holy, holy, holy, Lord
God Almighty, which was, and is, and is to come" (Rev.
4:8).

The word *beast* is a poor translation for us, though it
was accurate when the King James translation was
made. Then *beast* meant a living thing as opposed to an
inanimate thing. Today it means an animal as opposed
to a man, which is not the meaning in the above verse.
These *beasts* are four "living creatures" (RSV).

The living creatures' proclamation indicates the first
great unity—the person of God: He is eternal and he is
holy. In the book of Revelation this proclamation is a
future reality, but his existence and character remain un-
changed forever.

The New Theologians tend to say that the word *holy*
simply means the "godness" of God. But the Bible does
not use it like this. God's holiness includes his concern
228 about how men treat the moral law of the universe, the
law which is rooted in his own character. And in that
great future day, the living creatures will state that God
has eternal existence and that he is holy. But this is not
just a future thing; his existence and his holiness are
present realities as well.

The Second Great Unity: God Created All Things
Revelation 4:11 contains another statement of praise.
The first part of this overflowing verse says: "Thou art
worthy, O Lord, to receive glory and honour and power:
for thou hast created all things." We should not be surprised that the best Greek texts add the phrase "thou
art worthy, our Lord *and our God*," for we constantly find
paeans of praise being addressed to both the Father and
the Son. The text may be addressed to both the Father
and the Son, or it may be calling Christ our God. This
praise is not a shared glory, honor and power, but in the
Greek a definite article is used; it is *the* glory, *the* honor,

the power. In reality, there is no other final glory, honor and power. You are worthy to receive this, our Lord and our God, because of who you are.

The specific reason for praise in this case is that God has created all things. The Authorized Version does not give the text's emphasis. The sentence would be better translated, "for thou hast created all things, and because of thy will they were, and were created." Or, as the RSV says, "by thy will they existed and were created." The text is stressing that God did not need to create. He created everything because he *willed* to create. He spoke and it was.

God alone is the Creator. Everything there is, apart from the Trinity itself, whether the largest star in the universe or the smallest part of the atom, whether alive or inanimate, whether rational or merely conscious, whether in the seen or the unseen world, whether far off or near, stands as a created thing. This is the second great unifier of the past, present and future. God created the whole universe—angels, men, everything. God is Creator—non-created and infinite; all else is creature—created and finite. All else is dependent; all else depends upon God for its existence. This will be declared in that future time, but this also unites all that exists in space and time. He created all things, and he created me.

229

The Third Great Unity: Man Revolted against God
After John heard praise to God, he looked and "saw a strong angel proclaiming with a loud voice, Who is worthy to open the book, and to loose the seals thereof?" (Rev. 5:2). This is the book of redemption, and it points us to a third great unity which binds the future with the present and past. This unity involves something that happened on this side of creation, namely, the rebellion of angels and of man. Somewhere in history, at some moments of the tick of the clock, angels and man

revolted against God, and sin entered the universe.

Consequently, we live today in an abnormal world. Sin and guilt have shattered the normal relationship between moral creature and holy Creator. For all eternity it can never be as though sin had not entered. No matter how far down into the corridor of eternity we look, the fact remains that man rebelled. Some people will be marred for eternity by their rebellion. Others who have returned to God will fellowship with him *not* on the basis of their having been created for that fellowship but upon the basis of another factor, that of redemption.

In addition to God's existence and character, in addition to his being the Creator of all, there is now a third unity, man's sin. The angels' and man's sin has changed history. Therefore, a question now unites the future with the past and present, the question of how to return to God. And that question is raised in Revelation 5: Who can open the book of redemption?

230

Who Can Open the Book?
When the question Who can open the book? was raised in heaven, "no man [literally, *no one*] in heaven, nor in earth, neither under the earth, was able to open the book, neither to look thereon. And I [John] wept much, because no man [no one] was found worthy to open and to read the book, neither to look thereon" (Rev. 5:3-4). No mere creature of yesterday, today or tomorrow, no man, no angel and no living creature from any place in the created universe can provide the redemption which fallen man needs.

This is indeed something to weep about. To understand the abnormality of man and the world which is under his dominion is to begin to cry, "Who can open the book of redemption?" And when we hear the answer in heaven, "No creature can open the book of redemption," if we have anything but a heart of stone and if our theological orthodoxy is anything but dead theology, we will be moved. Is not man's dilemma, his being a sinner in the presence of a holy God, a cause for tears? Tears in the future, as John contemplates what it would mean if no one opened the book. Tears for me today if I understand.

But an answer came: "And one of the elders saith unto me, Weep not: behold, the Lion of the tribe of Judah, the Root of David, hath prevailed to open the book, and to loose the seven seals thereof" (Rev. 5:5). Here is one who can help—the Lion of the tribe of Judah, the greater son of David. The very terms are overwhelming and pregnant with meaning.

For when I ask who he is, suddenly the whole past is spread before me. This is he of whom the Old Testament spoke, the greater son of David, the one in New Testament history whose incarnation the angel announced to Mary, the eternal Son of God, who was born as a man by virgin birth, who walked upon the earth and died on Calvary's cross, who rose from the dead and who ascended into heaven. This has not happened in our heads; it has happened in past history. And in future history he is coming again. His past work, his continuing present presence and his future coming are bound together. Do not weep, for though no created being can open the book of redemption, there is one who can help: the Lion of the tribe of Judah. This is he who can help.

The Lamb of God

After John was told that someone could open the book, he saw the scene Van Eyck later attempted to portray in his marvelous *Adoration of the Lamb,* one of the world's great paintings: "And I beheld, and, lo, in the midst of the throne and of the four living creatures, and in the midst of the elders, stood a Lamb though it had been slain" (Rev. 5:6). Van Eyck, working with the limitations of his medium, pictures a lamb standing upon an altar with blood shooting forth from his wounded breast. In the future day Revelation portrays, there will be reality to this: The Lamb of God, slain in past history, will be standing erect. He is the slain one yet even now he lives, today and in that future day. Who is he? The Old Testament promised Messiah, slain yet living!

The lamb was central to the Old Testament sacrificial worship, and the didactic portions of the Old Testament, for example Isaiah 53, speak of Jesus' coming and his redemptive work. If we ourselves are redeemed, someday in the future space-time history we shall see him face to face and shall salute him as *our* Lamb. Our being in communication with God during Christ's millenial reign and into all eternity will rest exclusively upon Christ's past work as the Lamb of God. This is something that never will pass away. We will remember and celebrate Christ's death which destroyed death. Christ the Lamb opens the way to God. This will be true forever, and it is a reality that unites the past, present and future.

When the elders in heaven saw Jesus take the book of redemption, they sang "a new song, saying, Thou art worthy to take the book, and to open the seals thereof: for thou wast slain, and hast redeemed us to God by thy blood out of every kindred, and tongue, and people, and nation" (Rev. 5:9). Can you see the people in Van Eyck's painting streaming toward the Lamb from the north, south, east and west—people well-clothed in precious garments and people in poor garments, people with yellow skins, black skins, white skins. There are judges, knights, hermits and pilgrims. Watch them come, but remember that every one of them will be there on only one basis, Christ's death in history as the Lamb of God.

During the transfiguration, one of the last great prophetic acts before the death of Christ, Moses and Elijah met with Jesus, and only one subject of conversation was worthy of that great moment: Moses, Elijah and Jesus conversed about Jesus' coming death in Jerusalem. Only one subject could fill that moment because Moses and Elijah themselves had rested their hope of eternal salvation on the day soon to come. We who live on this side of the cross will understand more fully when we see God face to face than we can now that which rests upon the fact that the Lamb of God has been slain.

Kings and Priests
Revelation goes on to speak of a reality for which Christians do not have to wait: Christ has already made us "kings and priests" (or "a kingdom and priests") unto God (Rev. 5:10). In the millenial era, "we shall reign on the earth" (Rev. 5:10) with Jesus Christ in a way quite different from our Christian life now. But in certain ways this reign will be like our present experience of 233 the kingdom and priesthood.

It is again unity and diversity; for while it will be different then, a Christian in the present era is to show that he is a king under God, reigning well over the rest of God's creation. If men only did this, what a difference in ecology it would make. He is to exhibit he is a part of the kingdom now by showing that Christ is his present king. He is also to be a priest, giving his life to God which is a reasonable sacrifice (Rom. 12:1). Hebrews mentions two of the forms this can take: the sacrifice of praise to God and the sacrifice of sharing our wealth with brothers and sisters in Christ (Heb. 13:15-16). Giving is not to be something harsh and impersonal, merely the fulfilling of a technical duty. It is to be a priestly act in the presence of God and men.

Each Christian must thus remember that he is now a king and a priest. Though our environment in the future will be different, our calling is not totally different now.

Singing the Praises of God

After hearing the new song, John listened to another hymn of praise:

And I beheld, and I heard the voice of many angels round about the throne and the living creatures and the elders: And the number of them was ten thousand times ten thousand, and thousands of thousands (that is, endless numbers); Saying with a loud voice, Worthy is the Lamb that was slain to receive the power, and the riches, and wisdom, and strength, and honour, and glory, and blessing. And every created thing which is in heaven, and on the earth, and under the earth, and such as are in the sea, and all that are in them, heard I saying, the Blessing, and the honour, and the glory, and the power, be unto him that sitteth upon the throne, and unto the Lamb forever and ever. And the four living creatures said, Amen. And the four and twenty elders fell down and worshipped him that liveth for ever and ever. (Rev. 5:11-14)

234

In this future moment the voices of multitudes of angels, living creatures and men will praise Christ for the redemption he purchased not only for the Christian but for creation. The lion and the lamb, the little child and the asp; it is a redemption of all creation. This doxology is Bach cubed and carried to the nth power. Do we thrill now as we sing the praises of God in the tremendous music of Bach (who could write on his score "Glory to the Lamb")? Then how much more will we thrill when myriads of myriads, all of creation itself in song, each thing on its own level of creation, shout forth the wonder of the redemption purchased by the Lamb of God.

Though creation will be redeemed at that time in a way it is not today, we Christians now—before the redemption of creation, before the perfection of the church and before our own individual perfection—have exactly the same corporate and individual calling as these multitudes. Again it is unity in diversity. We are now to sing the praises of God, to declare and show forth that God really exists, to demonstrate that his character is holiness and love, to show the fruit of the work of Jesus Christ as the Lamb of God. This is the church's calling; basically it has no other.

God has not called the church to activism or only to organization but to let Christ bear his fruit through it, so that what will be shouted in such glory in the future will be spoken in the present world as well, not spoken as perfectly as then but spoken nevertheless. There is diversity in that the praise will not now be perfect as it will then be, but unity in that our lives individually and corporately should make the same statement today that will be made in that day.

In this present life, the church of Jesus Christ should be extolling God's glory with a great voice (v. 12). But all **235** too often we only hear it speaking very softly. If we listen with great care, we can just barely hear praise being given. But our calling is to speak forth by faith with a great voice! In certain periods, the church has spoken with a great voice. Now we long for it to speak this way again.

What are we to sing? Worthy is the Lamb that was slain, worthy is he to receive the power, and the riches, and the wisdom, and the strength, and the honor, and the glory, and the blessing. The blessing, and the honor, and the glory, and the power, be given to him that sits on the throne, and to the Lamb forever and ever. Amen.

John saw the twenty-four elders fall down and worship (v. 14) as an event in the future. But this event is not separated from the present. We Christians are to be filled with worship today.

In the art museum in Neuchatel are Paul Robert's murals of the second coming of Christ, probably the greatest ever made on this subject. In one picture, he portrays people inside a watch factory just before Christ's return. Most of them are worshipping wealth, but one group is different. This group is a joyful doxology to God in the midst of a lost and sad world.

One day all Christians will join in a doxology and sing God's praises with perfection. But even today, individually and corporately, we are not only to *sing* the doxology but to *be* the doxology.

The Wrath of the Lamb

Another section in Revelation links the present to the future:

And the kings of the earth, and the great men, and the rich men, and the chief captains, and the mighty men, and every bondman, and every free man, hid themselves in the dens and in the rocks of the mountains; And said to the mountains and rocks, Fall on us, and hide us from the face of him that sitteth on the throne, and from the wrath of the Lamb: For the great day of his wrath is come; and who shall be able to stand? (Rev. 6:15-17)

The dramatic event portrayed above will occur in the future because not all people are redeemed, but we must not forget that the wrath of the Lamb is also a present reality.

The wrath of the Lamb. What a strange term if we do not understand the structure of Scripture! The Lamb who died so that no man need be under the condemnation of God is the administrator of the wrath of God. The people ask the mountains to hide them "from the face of him that sitteth on the throne, and from the wrath of the Lamb," which demonstrates that both the Father and the Son are involved.

If we do not accept this, we do not believe in the God of Scripture. God is a God of love, but he is also a holy

God. All things contrary to his character are separated from him. So when I sin, I rebel against the law of the universe, which rests on the character of God, and I am justly pronounced *guilty*.

In the Gospel according to John is a verse God has used to lead many people to salvation: "He that believeth on the Son has everlasting life: and he that believeth not the Son shall not see life; but the wrath of God abideth on him" (John 3:36). This indicates that the wrath of God is already on the unbeliever, and it simply stays on him. There is no change; nothing turns it aside.

In the verse from John the Greek word for *wrath* is exactly the same as in the verse from Revelation. The word is used later in Revelation when John describes the wrath of the Lamb with strong words as Jesus comes in judgment: "And out of his mouth goeth a sharp sword, that with it he should smite the nations: and he shall rule them with a rod of iron: and he treadeth the wine press of the fierceness and wrath of Almighty God" (Rev. 19:15).

This, too, describes a present as well as a future reality, for the holiness of God is unchanging. A person cannot rationalize away or turn aside from the words Christ spoke while on the earth. While in London some time ago I saw a television program on the BBC; a well-known liberal theologian was speaking to two men who were not Christians in any sense. As they questioned him, he tried extremely hard to get rid of the words of Jesus that show the holiness of God's character and his judgment. But these words cannot be eliminated. When Jesus was on earth, he uttered words of judgment as well as words of love, comfort and invitation.

Can't we understand? Not all people are redeemed.

And why isn't everyone redeemed? Because not all have "washed their robes, and made them white in the blood of the Lamb" (Rev. 7:14). This will be a future event but it is related to the present too in regard to all the redeemed. The distinction is this: Those who are fellowshipping with God are doing so because they are "white in the blood of the Lamb."

Look closely at the description of the multitudes in Revelation 7:14: "These are they which came out of great tribulation, and have washed their robes, and made them white in the blood of the Lamb." Notice the verse says that they made them white in the blood of the Lamb. They, as true persons in significant history, made a choice. They believed God, and in so doing, they made their robes white in the blood of the Lamb. They are no longer under the judgment of God.

Christ has opened the book of redemption, but there is no other way an individual can share in it than making a choice based on the promises of God. In the past, Abraham and others looked forward to the coming of the Messiah. In our own era, we look back to the finished work of Christ. In the future, everyone who comes to God will look back in this same way. I would say again what the Bible says so clearly: There is no other way.

You, you who are reading this essay, have you made your robe white in the blood of the Lamb?

And if you have, as a Christian, are you following your priestly calling now, in the present?

Together—you and I and our Christian brothers and sisters—are we saying corporately with a great voice, "Worthy is the Lamb that has been slain to receive the power and riches and wisdom and might and honor and glory and blessing and worship"?

Revelation tells us that in the future we will know perfection: "For the Lamb which is in the midst of the throne shall be their shepherd and shall lead them unto living fountains of waters: and God shall wipe away all tears from their eyes" (Rev. 7:17). As men today look at those of us who comprise the kingdom and are the priests of God, can they see that we are being led by the Lamb who is the Shepherd? Can they see some evidence in the present that we are partaking of the fountain of life? Do our lives lift up a doxology to the Lord of the past, present and future? Does what will be true in the future absolutely have an observable reality now?

XV

What
Is
Enough?

Wh: does God require? What is enough to please him? Is it enough to speak certain words? or to affiliate with a certain group of people?

We must begin our answer to *What is enough?* with the understanding that using the "word" *God* is not sufficient. Consider the first portion of the Ten Commandments:

> And God spake all these words, saying, I am the LORD thy God, which have brought thee out of the land of Egypt, out of the house of bondage. Thou shalt have no other gods before me. Thou shalt not make unto thee any graven image, or any likeness of anything that is in heaven above, or that is in the earth beneath, or that is in the water under the earth: Thou shalt not bow down thyself to them, nor serve them: for I the LORD thy God am a jealous God, visiting the iniquity of the fathers upon the children unto the third and fourth generation of them that hate me; and shewing

mercy unto thousands of them that love me, and keep my commandments. Thou shalt not take the name of the LORD thy God in vain; for the LORD will not hold him guiltless that taketh his name in vain. (Ex. 20:1-7)

Verse 7—you shall not use the name of the LORD your God in vanity, or falsely—reminds us that verbalizing the word *God* is not in itself enough. The word is easily misused. We can displease God by swearing. But we can displease him just as much by using his name lightly. As biblical scholars have long recognized, the word *God* as used in the Ten Commandments represents God, so we might as well curse and swear as to use his name with a lack of reverence.

We can also misuse God's name by applying it to an idol. The first portion of the Decalogue makes clear that no "graven image," no idol, is to be made. But the text cuts even more deeply: "Thou shalt have no other gods before me." In other words, God requires more than that we refrain from using his name lightly or applying it to idols. He requires us to think of him as unique in both his existence and his character. We must recognize that he is there to speak.

God exists but there is more than the bare fact that some thing is there, for he is the self-revealer of his character as well as of his existence. And he has rooted his revelation of himself both in his actions in space-time history and in the commands of the law. He wants us to affirm the exclusiveness he has revealed. He is exclusive as God in regard to both his existence and his character. And he has revealed these things to us in a way we can comprehend and can discuss among the children of men. It is not enough to use the word *God* without the proper content.

The Golden Calf
The Ten Commandments give us positive teaching

about using the name of God. Then in Exodus 32 we are taught by a negative example:

> And when the people saw that Moses delayed to come down out of the mount, the people gathered themselves together unto Aaron, and said unto him, Up, make us gods, which shall go before us; for as for this Moses, the man that brought us up out of the land of Egypt, we do not know what is become of him. And Aaron said unto them, Break off the golden earrings, which are in the ears of your wives, and of your sons, and of your daughters, and bring them unto me. And all the people brake off the golden earrings which were in their ears, and brought them unto Aaron. And he received them at their hand, and fashioned it with a graving tool, after he had made it a molten calf: and they said, These be thy gods, O Israel, which brought thee up out of the land of Egypt. And when Aaron saw it, he built an altar before it; and Aaron made proclamation, and said, Tomorrow is a feast to the LORD. (Ex. 32:1-5)

In the final sentence of this quotation the Authorized Version capitalizes every letter in the word *LORD* because this word is the Tetragrammaton, the most holy name of God, which was so much at the center of Jewish worship that the Jews would not even pronounce it. They observed this custom for so long, in fact, that since they did not write down vowels in their language, eventually they forgot how to pronounce it. An inscription was placed upon the golden calf, and the Jews said, "These be thy gods, O Israel." This act was a deliberate violation of the Ten Commandments.

Notice that the word *God* was not absent. In fact, the name given to the golden calf was not merely that of some Canaanite deity. It was the name of the holy, covenant-keeping God—the Tetragrammaton, Jehovah. Tradition tells us (though this is not found in Scripture itself) that the Tetragrammaton was actually written on the golden calf's side or base. The calf was thus marked: "This is Jehovah."

Obviously, the use of the right word in this case was not enough. Using it broke both the command not to apply it to a "representation" and the command not to speak it in a way that would deny the exclusiveness that God had given of himself and his character. His character which he had revealed to them was violated by being interwoven with what occurred: "And they rose up early on the morrow, and offered burnt offerings, and brought peace offerings; and the people sat down to eat and to drink, and rose up to play" (Ex. 32:6).

And [after Moses and Joshua had started down the mountain] when Joshua heard the noise of the people as they shouted, he said unto Moses, There is a noise of war in the camp. And he said, It is not the voice of them that shout for mastery, neither is it the voice of them that cry for being overcome; but the noise of them that sing do I hear. And it came to pass, as soon as he came nigh unto the camp, that he saw the calf, and the dancing. (Ex. 32:17-19)

Arnold Schonberg did not misinterpret this scene in his opera *Moses and Aaron* when he portrayed it as a great orgy. Surrounded by heathen cultures in which it was normal to interweave sexuality with worship, the Israelites were not kept from this sin by using the right name of God, the Tetragrammaton. They totally destroyed the character of God as he had portrayed it in the Ten Commandments and in his exposition of them in other parts of the law.

Undoubtedly, many have attended Schonberg's opera to see the orgy and have become caught up in it themselves. These people, too, hear the name of God repeated again and again, but that does not save them from doing violence to the character of God as they sit in the opera house. Merely hearing and using the right word *God* is not enough.

God was angry not only because the children of Israel had built an idol. If they had applied the Tetragrammaton to the orgy alone (which they could have done even without erecting an idol), this would have broken the character of God just as completely; it would have brought them just as much under the wrath of God. Two factors are involved—the making of the idol and the orgy by which they violated the character of God as he had himself revealed it.

Using God's name did not save the Jews from breaking the character of God nor did it rescue them from the anger of Moses: "And Moses' anger waxed hot, and he cast the tables out of his hands, and brake them beneath the mount" (Ex. 32:19). The physical tablets might as well be broken because the commands they contained had already been broken by what the Jews had done. Moses' anger here is nowhere reproved by God. Moses had something to be angry about. The Tetragrammaton had been brought down not only to the level of a molten idol but also into a place of polluted worship.

245

Nor did it save them from the anger of God:

And the LORD said unto Moses, Go, get thee down; for thy people, which thou broughtest out of the land of Egypt, have corrupted themselves: they have turned aside quickly out of the way which I commanded them: they have made them a molten calf, and have worshipped it, and have sacrificed thereunto, and said, These be thy gods, O Israel, which have brought thee up out of the land of Egypt. And the LORD said unto Moses, I have seen this people, and, behold, it is a stiffnecked people: now therefore let me alone, that my wrath may wax hot against them, and that I may consume them. (Ex. 32:7-10)

Using the word *God* was not enough to deliver the people from the wrath of Moses nor, far more profoundly, from the wrath of God.

Jeroboam and the Two Golden Calves

There are many incidents in the Old Testament like that on Mount Sinai. One occurred at a crucial time soon after the division of the empire:

> And Jeroboam said in his heart, Now shall the kingdom return to the house of David: If this people go up to do sacrifice in the house of the LORD at Jerusalem, then shall the heart of this people turn again unto their lord, even unto Rehoboam king of Judah, and they shall kill me, and go again to Rehoboam king of Judah. Whereupon the king took counsel, and made two calves of gold, and said unto them, It is too much for you to go up to Jerusalem: behold thy gods, O Israel, which brought thee up out of the land of Egypt. And he set the one in Beth-el, and the other put he in Dan ... and Jeroboam ordained a feast in the eighth month, on the fifteenth day of the month, like unto the feast that is in Judah. (1 Kings 12:26-29, 32)

Notice that Jeroboam repeated the very words involved in the worship of the golden calf. The feast paralleled one given by God through Moses.

The tension in this situation again involved something more than idol worship. Verse 33 says Jeroboam changed the worship from what God had commanded to what he himself had conceived "in his heart" in humanistic flow out of himself. Jeroboam used the word *God*, but, as we would expect, God was not satisfied merely by Jeroboam's verbalization. He sent a prophet to tell Jeroboam what the punishment would be:

> And behold, there came a man of God out of Judah by the word of the LORD unto Beth-el: and Jeroboam stood by the altar to burn incense. And he cried against the altar in the word of the LORD, and said, O altar, altar,

246

thus saith the LORD; Behold, a child shall be born unto the house of David, Josiah by name; and upon thee shall he offer the priests of the high places that burn incense upon thee, and men's bones shall be burnt upon thee. And he gave a sign the same day, saying, This is the sign which the LORD hath spoken; Behold, the altar shall be rent, and the ashes that are upon it shall be poured out. And it came to pass, when king Jeroboam heard the saying of the man of God, which had cried against the altar in Beth-el, that he put forth his hand from the altar, saying, Lay hold on him. And his hand, which he put forth against him, dried up, so that he could not pull it in again to him. The altar also was rent, and the ashes poured out from the altar, according to the sign which the man of God had given by the word of the LORD. (1 Kings 13:1-5)

God communicated the same thing here as he did in response to the golden calf: To speak the name of God is not enough. God's wrath was laid upon the situation—not because Jeroboam did not use the word *God,* but because he applied the word in the wrong way. The word *God* isn't enough.

Jesus' Teaching

Jesus' teaching continues in exactly the same vein. He says to his disciples, "They shall put you out of the synagogues: yea, the time cometh, that whosoever killeth you will think that he doeth God service" (John 16:2). The final verb in this statement actually means to *offer*: Those who kill you or put you out of the synagogue will think they are making an *offering* to God.

And why? "These things will they do unto you," Jesus answers, "because they have not known the Father, nor me" (John 16:3). People know and use the word *God* but not its content. And having a content which is wrong, they can take the people of God and put them out of the synagogue; they can take the Son of God and hammer him to the cross.

It is perfectly possible to use the word *God* and yet under the umbrella of that word, hate the God who is. For Jesus said, "If I had not done among them the works which none other man did, they had not had sin: but now have they both seen and hated both me and my Father (John 15:24).

An even stronger statement is found in John 8, where Jesus again makes clear that the word *God* is meaningless unless one considers its content:

Ye do the deeds of your father. Then said they to him, We be not born of fornication; we have one Father, even God. Jesus said unto them, If God were your Father, ye would love me: for I proceeded forth and came from God; neither came I of myself, but he sent me. Why do ye not understand my speech? even because ye cannot hear my word. Ye are of your father the devil. (John 8:41-44)

Can't you hear the jangling of the music at the golden calf?

So whether our understanding is couched in the terms of the Old Testament or of Jesus' teaching, we see that speaking the word *God* is by no means enough to please the God who is.

The Name Christ or Jesus Is Not Enough

It is equally insufficient for someone just to use the name *Christ* or *Jesus*. In Galatians, a letter written about the so-called Judaizers in the early church, the apostle Paul says,

I marvel that ye are so soon removed from him that called you into the grace of Christ unto another gospel: Which is not another; but there be some that trouble you, and would pervert the gospel of Christ. But though we, or an angel from heaven, preach any other gospel unto you than that which we have preached unto you, let him be accursed. As we said before, so say I now again, If any man preach any other gospel unto you than that ye have received, let him be accursed. (Gal. 1:6-9)

In one of the strongest statements in the Word of God outside of the teaching of Jesus himself, Paul insists that the name *Christ* is not enough. The Judaizers had a gospel, but it was "another gospel." Just as the worshippers of the golden calf had another god—another god under the name God—here is another Christ under the name *Christ* and another gospel under the name *gospel*. This passage reminds us of the time Moses in his anger after he saw the golden calf threw down the tables and broke them. Paul confronted the churches of Galatia and said, "Because this 'gospel' is 'another gospel,' it is *no* gospel. Because it is not the gospel which accurately reveals the character of God and Christ, those who teach it are accursed." The Judaizers' gospel misrepresented God's character just as thoroughly as had the golden calf. With the golden calf, God's character became wrapped up with Canaanite worship. With the other "gospel," it became wrapped up with the humanistic worship which surrounded the Jews throughout the Mediterranean world—worship that allowed a man to come into the presence of God on the basis of his own works. **249**

To say the words *Christ* or *Jesus* or *gospel* does not help anybody. The Lord Jesus taught that many "christs" would come. The words must contain the content God himself has given about who Christ is, what Christ has done, and therefore what the gospel is.

An Ecclesiastical Relationship Is Not Enough

Being a citizen of Christendom or a member of a church is not enough either. Jesus gave a parable which applies to those today who merely use the name *Christ* in the midst of church and culture:

When once the master of the house is risen up, and hath shut to the door, and ye begin to stand without, and to knock at the door, saying, Lord, Lord, open unto us; and he shall answer and say unto you, I know you not whence ye are: Then shall ye begin to say, We have eaten and drunk in thy presence, and thou hast taught in our streets. But he shall say, I tell you, I know you not whence ye are; depart from me, all ye workers of iniquity. (Lk. 13:25-27)

Citizens of contemporary Christendom could ask the Lord many questions: Haven't you walked in our streets? Haven't you shaped our culture by the Reformation mentality? Haven't we shared in the peripheral blessings which have flowed from the Reformation? Isn't your name on billboards all across our nation? And to these questions the Lord Jesus would answer solemnly, "This type of relationship is not enough. Living in Christendom in no way guarantees to you God's approval."

But perhaps being a member of a professing church as a thing in itself pleases him. Consider this parable:

Then shall the kingdom of heaven be likened unto ten virgins, which took their lamps, and went forth to meet the bridegroom. And five of them were wise, and five were foolish. They that were foolish took their lamps, and took no oil with them ... and while they went to buy, the bridegroom came; and they that were ready went in with him to the marriage: and the door was shut. Afterward came also the other virgins, saying, Lord, Lord, open to us. But he answered and said, Verily I say unto you, I know you not. (Mt. 25:1-3, 10-12)

No, not everyone in the professing church will be saved and accepted by Christ. It is not enough to use the name of *God* or the name of *Christ* or to be in the visible church.

What Is Enough?

Well, then, what is enough to please God? We can find the answer in John 9, in the story of the man born blind. After this man had been given his sight, he testified to the Jewish leaders, "Whether he [Jesus] be a sinner or no, I know not: one thing I know, that, whereas I was blind, now I see" (John 9:25). Something had happened in this man's life—not merely an existential experience or a psychological miracle (he had been born blind!) but something involving verifiable data. His eyes had been opened.

"Then they [the Jewish leaders] reviled him, and said, Thou art his disciple; but we are Moses' disciples" (John 9:28). The leaders called themselves Moses' disciples (they had the right words), and yet they were capable of putting Christ out of the synagogue. On the other hand, this one man defended Christ, even calling him a prophet (John 9:17), and his declaration put him in sharp tension with these men who spoke the name *Moses*.

But the healed man himself needed something more. When "Jesus heard that they had cast him out; and when he had found him, he said unto him, Dost thou believe on the Son of God?" (John 9:35).

Some texts have "the Son of man" in Jesus' question, but this is no problem. In the first place, there is textual weight on the side of using "the Son of God." Far more important is the fact that the question parallels other passages in John. When Jesus was speaking to Nicodemus, Jesus did not tell Nicodemus how to be born again until he had told him about his own person, about who he was (John 3:13). Jesus did not ask the woman at the well to do anything until he had told her the content of who he was as the Old Testament-prophesied Christ

251

(John 4:25-26).

The parallelism between Jesus' conversation with the woman at the well and his interaction with the man born blind is especially strong. Both the claims he made in identifying himself and the results of the conversations are exactly parallel. When Jesus told the woman at the well, "I that speak with thee am he," she believed and passed the information on to everyone in her town, and they worshipped Jesus as the Christ, the Savior (John 4:42). When Jesus answered the man born blind, "Thou hast both seen him and it is he that talketh with thee" (John 9:37), the man fell down and worshipped. There would have been no reason for him to worship if Jesus had merely used the term *a son of man* in the weak sense.

This man who had been healed and had even elevated Jesus to the level of prophet needed additional content if the blessing he received from Jesus' hand was not to end at physical healing but was to continue on to salvation. When Jesus identified himself as the Son of God, the man responded, "Lord, I believe" (John 9:38). And the content of his belief is shown in the phrase "and he worshipped him" (John 9:38).

John, in his first letter, gives a test for discerning true spirits and prophets from false ones—a test which parallels the experience of the man born blind:

Beloved, believe not every spirit, but try the spirits whether they are of God: because many false prophets are gone out into the world. Hereby know ye the Spirit of God: Every spirit that confesseth that Jesus Christ is come in the flesh is of God: and every spirit that confesseth not that Jesus Christ is come in the flesh is not of God. (1 John 4:1-3)

The spirits and prophets are to be tested by whether they confess that Jesus "is come in the flesh," a confession that has two elements of content. It affirms both that Jesus existed before and also that he has come in the flesh. In other words, spirits and prophets must acknowledge both Jesus' pre-existence and his incarnation.

How are we, then, to test the spirits? the prophets? a strong emotion? all experience? There is only one way: on the basis of the *content* God has given.

John's test was not new. The Jews who read his letter would have been reminded of a test God had given in the Pentateuch:

> What thing soever I command you, observe to do it: thou shalt not add thereto, nor diminish from it. If there arise among you a prophet, or a dreamer of dreams, and giveth thee a sign or a wonder, And the sign or the wonder come to pass, whereof he spake unto thee, saying, Let us go after other gods, which thou hast not known, and let us serve them; Thou shalt not hearken unto the words of that prophet, or that dreamer of dreams. (Deut. 12:32—13:1-3)   253

God commanded the people to kill any prophet who sought to lead them away from the true God. And how were they to identify him? Just as in 1 John 1: Did he adhere to the content and commandments God had already given in Scripture? It made no difference whether that prophet gave a "prophecy" which came true or worked a miracle. It made no difference if the prophet gave rise to strong emotions within. If he contradicted the content of God's revelation, he was a false prophet.

But, while giving these negative commands, both 1 John and Deuteronomy confront us with what *is* enough to please God. What is enough is believing a content that can be known on the basis of God's revelation of himself, that which he has revealed in space-time history, that which can be truly and reasonably comprehended from the Scripture.

And the man born blind demonstrates this. Here was a man different from many of the people we have considered—those who used the word *God* at the golden calf, the Judaizers who spoke the name *Christ*, people today who are just citizens in Christendom and just members of churches. In distinction to all of these, this man, at the end of his encounter with Jesus, did that which is enough. When Jesus said, "Dost thou believe on the Son of God?" the man asked, "Who is he, Lord?" And when Jesus answered, "Thou hast both seen him and it is he that talketh with thee," the man responded, "I believe," and worshipped Jesus.

I, too, need to do this. I need to know God truly in his self-revealed existence and character. I need to know the real Christ in his person and finished work. I need a right relationship with the God who is really there. In short, like the man born blind, I need a right relationship with Christ as my Savior and with the living God as my God.

254   Nothing short of this is enough.

XVI

Ash
Heap
Lives

The world is afire. Not only do we face strenuous days now, but, if my projections are right, we can expect our times to become even more difficult. I think that God's people are about to enter a struggle unlike anything they have experienced for many generations. The next two to five decades will make the last few years look like child's play.

We Christians should be asking ourselves, "What must we do to speak effectively to such a world?" I believe with all my heart that in order to speak to this generation we must *act* like a Bible-believing people. We can emphasize a message faithful to the Bible and the purity of the visible church, but if we do not practice this truth we cannot expect anyone to listen to us.

Yet we must go on even deeper than this; we must go on to a Bible-centered spirituality. In the last chapter of *Death in the City*, I point out that each person sits in one of two chairs—either the naturalist chair or the supernaturalist chair—and he perceives everything in the universe from the perspective of that chair. When an individual is born again, he moves from the former chair to the latter. The tragedy is that even after a Christian has affirmed the supernatural it is perfectly possible for him, in practice, to move back to the naturalist chair and spend most of the rest of his life there, seeing things from the same perspective as the world and living on the same basis. If a man does not believe the promises of God for salvation, we say he is in *unbelief*. The position of a Christian who sits in the naturalist chair is what I call *unfaith*. Many Christians live much of their lives there. I wish to speak to this problem, not by stressing the positive aspects of spiritual things (I have done this in *True Spirituality*, *The Mark of the Christian* and at the end of *Death in the City*) but by dealing with the negative —the danger of materialism in a Christian's life.

258

Practical Materialism

Materialism can be understood in several ways. Those who are philosophically oriented will think of philosophic materialism. This perspective, which dominates our educational system today, is antithetical to Christianity. It says that man is only the energy particle more complex and that religion is no more than a psychological or sociological tool. So Christians reject this; they cannot be this sort of materialist.

Some people will think of the materialism represented by the communist philosophy and communist nations —dialectical materialism. And because it is horrible that these states limit the perspective of millions of people (especially the children) to an entirely materialistic explanation of life, as well as subordinate the individual to the state, Christians cry out, "Down with dialectical materialism!"

But even Christians can reject both of these materialisms and yet not escape from a third kind—what I call *practical materialism.* Tragically, all too many of us live out this antithesis of true spirituality. We all tend to live "ash heap lives"; *we spend most of our time and money for things that will end up in the city dump.*

Practical materialism is difficult to escape in any age, but it is especially hard today because we all tend to be influenced by the spirit around us, and in the United States and the western world most people have only two values—personal peace and affluence. Many young people have rejected their parents' style of materialism only to come round in a big circle to their own kind. As long as they have enough money to pay for their pad and feed their lifestyle, they care about nothing else.

Are Christians ever like this? I remember our first years on the "mission field" (1947-48). We came to a Europe filled with poverty-stricken people. In this setting were material possessions automatically an asset in missionary work? There were not many automobiles in Rome (perhaps happily, when we think of Rome today), but a missionary invited me into a big American car and drove me through the streets. How wrong he was to think that the impressive automobile, shipped over on a boat at great expense, landed on a dock at Genoa and driven to Rome, would automatically increase his effectiveness. It did not; it diminished it. His abuse of possessions was both unspiritual and insensitive. I left Rome thinking, "Here is real materialism."

Spain, too, was bitterly poor. With the exception of a very few wealthy, most people's lives were dreadful. Yet I was invited to a missionary's apartment which was overwhelmingly luxurious—not, perhaps, in comparison to what this same man would have had as a pastor in America but exceedingly affluent by Spanish standards then. He said to me, "I don't understand it, but we seem separated from the people. There seems to be a wall be-

259

tween us and them." What do you think happened when he invited the poor people into his luxurious home to a Bible study? The effort was useless.

In Europe today, of course, this is not true. (Now everyone owns an automobile except the Schaeffers!) But there are still countries in the world where the Christians' use of money creates a "we-they" dichotomy. Such a situation cannot possibly lead people to believe that Christians are serious about trusting their Father in heaven and about sharing with their fellow men.

Do we understand that material possessions are not necessarily good in themselves even in this life? Let me give two illustrations from our early days in Switzerland. When we first came to the villages of Switzerland, most of the women washed their clothes at the village pumps. This was not just something staged for a tourist postcard. When I saw them walking down to the village fountain, putting their hands in the cold water and standing outside even in bad weather, my typical American reaction was: "Isn't this a shame? Wouldn't it be wonderful if these people had washing machines?" Gradually a different idea dawned on me—working at the fountain took up a lot of the woman's day, but she spent the time talking with other village women, doing a necessary job; she existed in a very human setting. Was that worse than a woman in the United States or a woman in Europe today who has a great number of labor-saving devices—who pops her dirty clothes into a washer and leaves them—but who spends all her time being morose and lonely? The question is, What does she do with the time she saves? If she spends all her time just doing nothing or destroying herself and her family, wouldn't she be better off washing at the village pump in the cold water?

Also, when I first came to Europe, many women worked in the field because farm machinery was scarce.

260

Even on the larger farms, most jobs had to be done by hand, and this was certainly true on the small Swiss farms. In those days, the work was hard. Now all the Swiss have lovely little tractors, made especially for the mountainsides. But then cutting the hay meant working the scythe by hand and loading the wagon. And I saw women out laboring with their husbands, sometimes doing the hard work of pitching the hay. I thought of all the American women who did not have to do this: "My, wouldn't it be wonderful if the Swiss women could be saved from this hard physical work?" But I have changed my mind completely. The women who worked with their husbands shoulder to shoulder during the day and then slept with them at night had one of the greatest riches in the world. Is anything worse than our modern affluent situation where the wife has no share in the real life of her husband?

Is it really true, then, that having increased material **261** possessions is automatically good even in this life? No. Of all people, Christians should know this because God's Word teaches it. We must not get caught up in practical materialism.

Laying Up Treasure

In seeing beyond the present life, a Christian's perspective is supposed to be different. We must never live in the perspective of this life alone but should affirm that our present existence has a horizontal extension into a life to come. The Bible tells us that a cause-and-effect relationship exists between what happens now and what happens in eternity. We are often told, "You can't take it with you." But this is not true. You can take it with you—if you are a Christian. The question is, Will we?

Jesus himself taught this: "Lay not up for yourselves treasures upon earth, where moth and rust doth corrupt, and where thieves break through and steal: But lay up for yourselves treasures in heaven, where neither moth nor rust doth corrupt, and where thieves do not break through nor steal" (Mt. 6:19-20).

This statement is to be taken literally. Jesus never uttered mere "God words." Liberal theologians with the concept of realized eschatology consider this only a way of stirring up motivation for the present life, but this is not the Bible's perspective. Jesus was not merely making a psychological adjustment inside a man's head. He was telling us that in actual fact we can lay up our treasure in one of two places. In one place, it will assuredly rot away; in the other, it will never decay. We can lay up money in land or investments, but we can lay it up just as realistically and objectively in heaven. It is as though Jesus had mentioned the First National Bank in New York as opposed to the Banque Suisse and said that you can choose to make your investments in either America or Switzerland. The perspective of our lives should be that we can lay up treasure in one of two places—earth or heaven.

Jesus emphasized this in a parable:
And he said unto them, Take heed, and beware of covetousness: for a man's life consisteth not in the abundance of the things which he possesseth. And he spake a parable unto them, saying, The ground of a certain rich man brought forth plentifully: And he thought within himself, saying, What shall I do, because I have no room where to bestow my fruits? And he said, This will I do: I will pull down my barns, and build greater; and there will I bestow all my fruits and my goods. And I will say to my soul, Soul, thou hast much goods laid up for many years; take thine ease, eat, drink, and be merry. But God said unto him, Thou fool, this night thy soul shall be required of thee: then whose shall those things be, which thou hast

provided? So is he that layeth up treasure for himself, and is not rich toward God. (Lk. 12:15-21)

These are strong words: A man is a fool to put money in a bank that is not going to last when he can deposit it in a bank that will.

Often this is used as an evangelistic text to point out that anyone is foolish who builds for this life while forgetting that one day he will have to stand before God in judgment. Undoubtedly this truth is involved here, but there is more. Jesus is not only speaking to the man who spends all of his time, as so many do, accumulating wealth with no thought of God. He is also addressing Christians. If we are acting like this, then either we do not really believe in the future life or we are fools for laying up money in a bank that can be plundered. Death will strip us of all the material possessions we leave upon this earth. Death is a thief. Five minutes after we die our most treasured possessions which are invested in this life are absolutely robbed from us. It is a terrible thing that many Christians read this passage year in, year out, and they never see that it applies to them.

Jesus summed all this up in yet another statement: "Sell that ye have, and give alms; provide yourselves bags which wax not old, a treasure in the heavens that faileth not, where no thief approacheth, neither moth corrupteth" (Lk. 12:33). Imagine a man who has to carry five thousand dollars over the Alps and who has a choice of two bags. One is made of cheesecloth, and he knows that if he uses it the money will soon begin dribbling out. So he chooses the other—a heavy leather bag. When he arrives at his destination the money is safe. Jesus is just as explicit: When we lay up our treasures in this life, we have chosen a worthless bag. We *are* going someplace, you know, and when we arrive we do not want to find we have left everything upon the way.

Notice that Jesus introduces the statement about bags

263

with a practical implication: "Sell that ye have, and give alms." The Scripture makes no distinction between giving to the needy and giving to missionary work. Often to the evangelical mind, money given to missions is the only money given to the Lord. Now, I am not minimizing contributing to missionary work. Christians do not do this enough. In fact, Christians in countries like the United States and Britain will have to answer to God for investing such a small amount in missions. But there is also a practical humanitarianism in the Scripture. Christians have the important job of meeting men's material needs as well as their personal and spiritual needs. The book of James is strong on just that point. If the church had practiced and preached this truth during and after the Industrial Revolution, we probably would not be in our current mess. Today we in the evangelical church in the affluent countries must understand and believe that we can lay up treasures in heaven both through our missionary giving and through other uses of our money to care for people and especially our fellow Christians.

264

There is a peculiar kind of capitalism in the Bible—a capitalism, an acquired property, that cares for people. And this we have forgotten. Our choice is not between a capitalism, an acquired property, which is hard, cold and unloving (characterized by people who care for nobody but themselves as they amass great fortunes) and a socialism in which the state owns everything. The Christian has a third option—property acquired and used with compassion.

Making Friends

Jesus had other things to say about the right use of possessions:

> And he said also unto his disciples, There was a certain rich man, which had a steward; and the same was accused unto him that he had wasted his goods. And

he called him, and said unto him, How is it that I hear this of thee? give an account of thy stewardship, for thou mayest be no longer steward. Then the steward said within himself, What shall I do? for my lord taketh away from me the stewardship: I cannot dig; to beg I am ashamed. I am resolved what to do, that, when I am put out of the stewardship, they may receive me into their houses. So he called every one of his lord's debtors unto him, and said unto the first, How much owest thou unto my lord? And he said, An hundred measures of oil. And he said unto him, Take thy bill, and sit down quickly, and write fifty. Then said he to another, And how much owest thou? And he said, An hundred measures of wheat. And he said unto him, Take thy bill, and write fourscore. And the lord commended the unjust steward, because he had done wisely: for the children of this world are in their generation wiser than the children of light. And I say unto you, Make to yourselves friends of the mammon of unrighteousness; that, when ye fail, they may receive you into everlasting habitations. (Lk. 16:1-9)

The steward's lord commended him not because he was unjust, but "because he had done wisely." Jesus applies this to you and me: "And I say to you, Make to yourself friends." How? By the wise use of your present riches. In other words, if you want to be wise, make friends by the way you use your money, so that when you die these friends who are then already in heaven will receive you into everlasting habitations. This is a realistic picture, not just an upper-story situation, a drug trip or something Jesus said only to enable people to bear their present problems.

If you are a Christian, you are really going to be in heaven, and some of the people you now know will be there, and they will speak with you about what you did in this life. Somebody will say to you, "Thank you so much for the money you gave me when my children were starving. I didn't have a chance to thank you then, but I do now." "I remember the night you opened your home to me, when you moved over and shared your table with me." This is what Jesus was saying, and he implied that you are a fool if you do not keep this in mind. This is taking our material possessions with us in a most practical manner. There is a horizontal continuity from this life to the life to come.

Jesus continued his commentary on the parable with these words,

> He that is faithful in that which is least is faithful also in much: and he that is unjust in the least is unjust also in much. If therefore ye have not been faithful in the unrighteous mammon, who will commit to your trust the true riches? And if ye have not been faithful in that which is another man's, who shall give you that which is your own? No servant can serve two masters: for either he will hate the one, and love the other; or else he will hold to the one, and despise the other. Ye cannot serve God and mammon. (Lk. 16:10-13)

The "true riches" obviously have nothing to do with money. To have spiritual power to overcome the awfulness of the post-Christian world—that is true riches. The church is constantly saying, "Where's our power? Where's our power?" Jesus' statement here gives us at least part of the answer. We must use money with a view to what counts in eternity. If a child cannot take his father's money, go to the store, purchase what is requested and return home with the change, it does not make sense for the father to increase his allowance. So since, like the steward in the parable, the money we handle is not our own, if we do not bring it under the lordship of Christ, we will not be given the greater wealth of spiritual power.

Some of his hearers did not readily accept Jesus' words: "The Pharisees also, who were covetous, heard all these things: and they derided him" (v. 14). These were men of the orthodox party—did they fight for their orthodoxy! Yet they laughed at Jesus because they did not want any part of this teaching. Let me say with tears that, as far as material possessions, time, energy and talents are concerned, all too many Bible-believing Christians live as though their entire existence is limited to this side of the grave.

We cannot ignore Jesus' statement about these two irreconcilable reference points: "You cannot serve God and riches" (Mt. 6:24). Either riches in this life, or the reality of God and the future—one of them *must* give the overshadowing cast to our lives. To the extent that wealth (or power) is our reference point, we are spiritually poor. If we were to plot this on a graph, as the line indicating the importance we place on possessions rises, a second line indicating spiritual reality plummets. We cannot expect the power of God if our reference point is the things of this world, for practical materialism and true spirituality have no affinity for one another.

Jesus summed all this up by saying, "For where your treasure is, there will your heart be also" (Mt. 6:21). Our decision about which bank we store our wealth in is a spiritual phenomenon! It is a piece of spiritual litmus paper or, to use another image, a spiritual thermometer. It tests the reality of our faith and indicates our spiritual health. If we are living only in the perspective of this life, our spiritual temperature is low indeed.

Imagine a man speaking about his retirement: "When I retire," he says, "I am going to live in such-and-such a house." He talks about this house incessantly, so much so that finally you decide to take a look at it. You are surprised to find it a shambles—with its shutters off, its windows broken and everything grown over. Would we

267

believe that the man really thought to retire there? Well, what about us? We say we are looking forward to heaven, but we let our heavenly home fall into ruins while we invest everything we have in a house that is not going to _ast. Why should people take us seriously when we claim we really believe we are going to be in heaven? What is involved is not just the amount of money we give to "the church." What is involved is the way we spend it all.

We have a right to spend money—do not misunderstand me and start feeling guilty for the wrong reasons. We are not automatically spiritual if we despise money. Many of the younger generation think they are superior if they simply despise wealth and things. We need clothes and food. There is a time to buy flowers and to take a vacation. What is important is not despising acquired wealth; it is using all our money wisely before the face of God.

On the Ash Heap

I lived in St. Louis before the city passed the smoke ordinances, so everybody had a concrete or brick dump in the back of his yard. As you walked in the front of the houses, they looked terrific; but as you walked through the alleys, you had to hold your nose. Inside these small, burning dumps one could see all the things people had spent their lives for.

Have you ever walked through a city dump? You should. When I was growing up in Philadelphia, I would hike every Saturday. To get to the clean air of the country I used to save a couple miles by tramping through the city dump. I have never forgotten this. It was a place of junk, fire, stench. It has helped me tremendously to think back on that place, because even as a boy I realized that I saw there almost everything people spend their money for. That was where their investment

ended. Some things may be handed down in a family
for five hundred years (though certainly most things you
buy today will not), but someday they will be gone.
Here is a topic for Christian artists or poets: "Meditation
on an Ash Heap" or "Ode on a City Dump."

Have you ever had to "break up" a rich man's house
after he has died? It is a sad thing to go through the
home of someone who has spent his entire life laying up
riches in this world. I recall one instance where a non-
Christian man had owned a large, gorgeous dining
room table. He had had it built inside his house and had
been very proud of it. When it came time to dispense his
household goods, there was no way to take the table
apart without spoiling it, so they simply took an axe,
chopped it up and threw the pieces on a fire. The admonition of Jesus had come to pass: The man had proven
himself a fool; his possessions were either destroyed or
carted away. How pathetic!   269

In our culture nothing has exhibited such folly more
than our automobiles. Go to a showroom and see the
pride with which a man drives out his new car. Then
think of an automobile graveyard or a rusting, stripped,
junked car, abandoned on a city street. They are shells
screaming out tremendous sermons against all practical
materialism: "You're fools! You're fools! You're fools!"
And Christians—as well as any others—can be such
fools with their wealth.

One experience vividly taught me this lesson. Edith
and I had had a Model A Ford. In it we had courted and
honeymooned. In it we had rushed to the hospital where
Priscilla was born. It was our car during our first pastor-
ate. It was precious to me, but after I had broken a spring
hauling youngsters to summer Bible school and was
driving up the street on a slant, the church decided it
was getting too ramshackled for their testimony, so they
asked me to get a new one. I was sad about my old auto-

mobile, I felt like a traitor, but the new car was tremendous! It was a brand new, secondhand Chevrolet. It was polished as only secondhand auto salesrooms polish cars. I have never been more filled with pride than when I left the showroom. But I did not get home before someone passed me too closely in a narrow alley and put a long scratch on the fender, and the joy was gone. But I am so glad it got scratched. That was one of the best things that ever happened to me, for suddenly I learned how much possessions stink if you look at them in the wrong perspective.

Tried by Fire
Christians should also keep in mind that their works will be judged. The apostle Paul described that judgment:

270
According to the grace of God which is given unto me, as a wise masterbuilder, I have laid the foundation, and another buildeth thereon. But let every man take heed how he buildeth thereupon. For other foundation can no man lay than that is laid, which is Jesus Christ. Now if any man build upon this foundation gold, silver, precious stones, wood, hay, stubble; Every man's work shall be made manifest: for the day shall declare it, because it shall be revealed by fire; and the fire shall try every man's work of what sort it is. If any man's work abide which he hath built thereupon, he shall receive a reward. If any man's work shall be burned, he shall suffer loss: but he himself shall be saved; yet so as by fire. (1 Cor. 3:10-15)

A Christian has only one foundation: Jesus Christ his Savior. And on that foundation he builds—with either combustible or non-combustible material. One day there will be a believers' judgment because we live in a moral universe and every book must be balanced in the presence of the holy Judge, and in that judgment the fire will come. I like to picture it as a great prairie fire which sweeps along burning everything in its path. Suddenly it comes to a great rock, leaps up over it and passes on. Everything on that rock which can be burned (the wood, hay and stubble) is consumed; everything that cannot be burned (the gold, silver and precious stones) stands for eternity. The Spirit inspired Paul to make it plain (and Paul knew the question would arise) that this does not concern salvation. The building may be destroyed but the builder still will live. The tragedy is that after we are born again, we can build upon the Rock things that are going to be consumed, so that after we have stood before the Lord Jesus Christ as Judge, we have little left. This is a danger not only to businessmen but to missionaries and ministers, not only to individuals but to congregations and organizations.

By God's grace, let us not be infiltrated by the values of affluence and personal peace. Let us use the treasures God has given us in such a way that when we come to that day we will have treasures laid up in heaven and people eagerly waiting for us.

271